AF565112

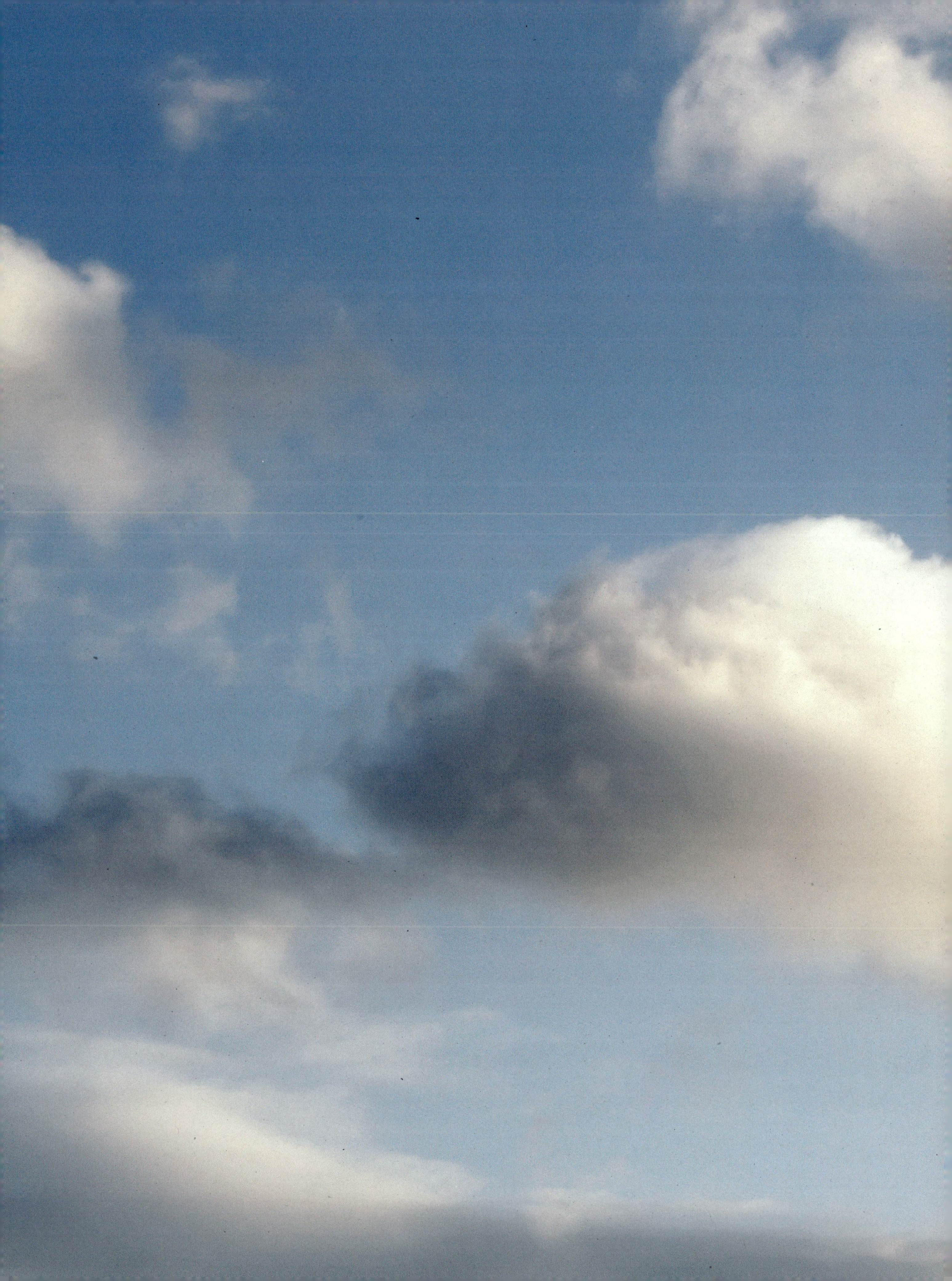

The Story behind "El Martillo"

"The hammer has been destroyed!" Artúr's excited voice cried out at the other end of the line. I ran over to the closest computer and logged onto the Yahoo web page, where I found a pixelated video clip from ITN News. I saw a solemn procession of masked men and women carrying a giant, shiny inflatable hammer, through the sunlit streets of Cancún. After giving us a look into the insides of a large conference hall, the clip returned to the parade. But now the unwritten ceremonial order had been broken: The group with the shining hammer was storming forward, towards a boarded up conference centre that looked more like a medieval castle than a meeting place for democratic politics. It was guarded by men dressed in blue and black uniforms with armor, and faceshields instead of faces.

A few seconds later the guardians of the Mexican government, the police, decapitated the hammer – our hammer! – with a sickening move of a hunter's knife, as if killing not a symbol but an animal.

I cannot even begin to describe the strangeness of watching these images, separated from the events not only by the Pacific Ocean, but also by the dull stupor of the media who repeatedly aired the same images, be it the German station ZDF or the Chinese Kang-Dynasty TV. Should I write that it was odd to see this object that we had worked so hard on be represented in two dimensions, in low-resolution on only a screen, yet admit with a certain satisfaction, that we had reached our goal? Relieved that it was finally over with? Once again, I return to insufficient words such as "odd" or "strange" which are nothing but empty place-holders for the confusing feeling of being happy over the destruction of your own artwork. How does one describe distance?

Maybe it was relief felt at seeing the results of a working process that drained out all of our energy throughout those months. It was also the end of a community of around 20 students, artists, theoreticians, activists, seamstresses and others who had come together in the OKK project space in Berlin-Wedding to build on a collective art piece for the 16th UN climate conference (COP 16) in Cancún.

But why a hammer? This was always the first question that we had to answer during interviews with the press. We would give a standard reply, but we always struggled with keeping our answers short. So bear with us.

The Eclectic Electric Collective was founded in 2008 in Glasgow and has since gone through many different constellations. At that time, Artúr and I were cooperating with a group of activists fighting against climate change by opposing the expansion of airports – aviation fuels being one of the most overlooked pollutants. For example, consider the fact that flying accounts for 13 % of all yearly U.K. Emissions (!).[1] Our cooperation with Plane Stupid Scotland and their blockade of an airport runway in Aberdeen in 2009 heightened our sensitivity to the issue, to such an extent, that we decided to travel 400 km to the UN COP 15 in Copenhagen in a group of three – in the middle of winter, on bicycles, Artúr, Su, and I. Our aversion to flying was also the original impulse for the "El Martillo" project, as we were facing the question of how we could make an impact on the COP 16 climate conference in Cancún, without having to hoist our bodies 10 000 meters into the air. The carbon footprint for one single person alone to fly between Berlin and Mexico City would amount to about 2,3 tons of carbon dioxide. We did not want to get involved in "summit hopping" without feeling like hypocrites.

Aside from coming home to Berlin with material from the COP 15 trip that would result in the production of a documentary film and an installation, we also came back with a profound realization of how political events can be turned into media spectacles. Whether being in large scale demonstrations or involved with direct action groups trying to regain power from the squabbling politicians of the world, sitting in their conference headquarters guarded by 5,000 policemen – we were constantly being followed. Followed by a third party, a group of people constantly carrying around telephones, cameras, microphones, helmets and press ID's that would get them out of trouble with pepper spray. The media. There were moments when we felt like there were more cameras than protesters, which in itself was quite an achievement considering how successful the mass mobilization had been all over Europe. Copenhagen was supposed to stand next to Seattle in the radical history books of the future as the birth place of a new green movement, taking over the flame of radical resistance from the anti-globalization movement. But things played out differently. The "movement of movements" was squashed through excessive police repression and mass waves of so-called "pre-emptive" arrests (the police arrest people whom they suspect of possibly committing a crime in the future), the politicians could not agree on even the most basic of levels – and everything was being followed by the eyes of the media.
And us.

Contrary to the journalists, though, we were aware of the fact that we were only creating narratives. We did not believe in any fairy tales of objectivity. Our narratives were not mirrors giving reality a good look at itself; our narratives were hammers, narratives that have the power to change reality as such.

During the planning process of the project, we hooked up with Pablo Herrmann, a politically engaged artist, who was running the project space OKK (Organ für kritische Kunst – Organ for critical Art) in Berlin-Wedding. Our original plan was to create enormous paintings in Muralismo style to be sent over to Mexico as banners. But as we were having one of our meetings, drinking tea and beer in Pablo's space, Rafael Ibarra, a Mexican muralist, came up with the idea that we should create inflatables instead. We all immediately jumped at the idea. A few weeks later we opened the doors of the OKK, set up a large dinner table for a potluck dinner and welcomed about 20 different people to the project. After the first couple of glasses of wine and plates of hummus, we started to actually work. During our first collective brainstorm someone remembered a quote being used commonly in anti-globalisation circles, commonly attributed to German playwright Bertolt Brecht: "Art is not a mirror held up to reality but a hammer with which to shape it."

The quote immediately struck our imagination, and we decided to give our inflatable the shape of a hammer. Its inherent symbolism left us with a feeling of ambivalence, which in itself was exciting. Researching the origins of the quote we realized, that, depending on the source, it has also been variously attributed to futurist poet Vladimir Mayakovsky and Karl Marx himself. The origins of the quote may be covered in mist, but there seemed to be a familiarity between Brecht, Mayakovsky and Marx. They were all children of the first generations of the worker's movements, during a period when Europe found itself in the middle of vast cultural upheaval, and as revolutionaries around the world still held the hope of installing a new political system, based on the equality of all humans alive, under the scarlet red flag of communism. This triggered us, not only because of its inherent utopian ideals, but also because of the thorny realities of the Soviet system. Some of us were second-generation immigrants from the Eastern Bloc who had experiences of having their parents fleeing the repression of the communist regimes, in order to find freedom in the capitalist West. Hence, the embodiment of our communist quote could be nothing but spiced with a bittersweet tinge of irony.

The end project was thus filled with ambiguities: from being a radical activist undertaking to protest the UN climate conference and metaphorically "stamp out the talks" (as the Reuters and ITN news presenter put it), as well as an artist project, that looked like it might have sprung out of the back pocket of Jeff Koons. Contrary to the opinion of some activists, we do not believe that a political action has to be one hundred percent straightforward in order to be effective. By embracing ambivalence and playfulness, one allows people to join a movement on their own terms, without being dogmatic. "El Martillo" is dead and alive. It created a community in Germany and Mexico and it lives on, as long as people remember it.

Hence, the purpose of this publication: This publication is a patchwork of the different contexts sewn together. It gives an insight into the climate justice movements of Mexico at the time of the UN climate conference in Cancún. At the same time it describes an artistic strategy, that subverts the current dominant imagery connected to the climate change discourse.[2] By sharing our collective process, both technically and theoretically, we hope to inspire artists and activists to cooperate with one another. For this reason we've included the following texts in this publication.

An important text for our collective was "The Phenomenology of Giant Puppets", written by anthropologist David Graeber. It was through this text that we started to understand the media impact giant puppets in political demonstrations could have, and envisioned how "El Martillo" could become a tool for empowering protestors.

What happened to "El Martillo", as it was taken through Mexico in a bus by the climate activist group Marea Creciente, is the topic of Cristian Guerrero's text "Fighting for the Air we Breathe." It gives an insight into the organization of the COP demonstrations, as social movements traveled in caravans through the country in order to make a critical stance against the neo-liberal policies negotiated at the climate conference in Cancún. In a transcript of our e-mail conversation he also explains how the hammer finally made it into the media through its own destruction, and how it managed to weld the group together during the tumultuous COP 16 protests, which were scarred by internal rivalry.

As a collective we believe that the material of an artwork should be society, the concept of "social sculpture", coined by Joseph Beuys. One of today's most interesting artists working in this tradition is the London based artist-activist John Jordan, co-founder of groups such as "Platform", "Reclaim the Streets" and "Laboratory of Insurrectionary Imagination." In the interview "Against Representation", he shares his views on the role of art in shaping society.

In the text "The Body of the Image, or towards a Communist Art Practice" the project itself is being discussed by critical theoretician Alex Dunst, who also participated in the building of the hammer. Emanating from a reinterpretation of the term "communism", he sees the hammer as an image, or body, of the protesters in Mexico and abroad, an image that stands in to the defense of the commons, but with an ironic distance to communism's tradition of instrumentalised violence.

In the "Manual" and the accompanying poster, Sarah Drain and Paul Pistorius have put together an easy-to-use set of instructions for how to build your own inflatable. The manual at the very end of the publication maps out the technical process of sewing a giant inflatable, whereas the poster functions as a blueprint. By following the steps mapped out in the manual, you will be able to create your very own hammer to take with you in a shopping trolley to the next demonstration.

A project like this would have been absolutely impossible without the dedication of the many amazing people involved. Without the collective, "El Martillo" would have been nothing more than a crackpot sketch, an idea, nothing but a bubble of words without substance. Of the many people involved, this introduction offers mostly the perspective of only one person, and what follows is only a humble, yet sincere attempt to acknowledge the incredible effort and input the following individuals have contributed.

First of all, we want to acknowledge Cristian Guerrero and all the amazing people of the Mexican climate activist group "Marea Creciente", without whom this project would have been a fart in the ocean. Unfortunately, we never had an opportunity to meet up in person, as the coordination was done through e-mails and skype, but the images and videos of the actions that Marea Creciente performed with the hammer filled us with pride.

Enough praise cannot be heaped upon Pablo Herrmann, our contact person at OKK, who enthusiastically supported the project. The collaboration with OKK was in many ways crucial to the project, as their network provided not only a space for us to build the hammer, but also because they helped organise the preparation of the workshop, the fundraising and the organisation of a subsequent exhibitions of the project. Aside from Pablo, we would also like to thank Juan-Pablo Arce, Marcelo Arteaga, Juan-Pablo Diaz and Ricardo Ramirez of the OKK crew.

During the making of the hammer, the Eclectic Electric Collective went through a constant flux of members. However there was a core of dedicated individuals whose presence was absolutely essential: Sarah Drain, a Hamburg based student of psychology and sewing specialist was absolutely invaluable to the project with her know-how and 24-hour commitment. Another participant in the hammer sewing workshop was Heather Purcell, a cheery artist from Liverpool who enlightened everyone's days during the sewing of the hammer with her work ethic and constant good mood. Without Rafael Ibarra we would have been doing murals, and they would have probably not been finished on time either. Others, such as Glasgow based artist Alex Misick, Berlin based artists, Melanie Schlachter, Latefa Wiersch, Hanna Moik, Anton Theileis, Jakub Theileis, Maria Nuebling, New York based artist Erika Ceruzzi and the Budapest based Csilla Hodi, Betti Tóth and Gábor Pinter were absolutely essential to the construction of the hammer and the installation of the ventilator.

Our gratitude goes out to Tadzio Müller, press spokesman for the climate activist groups Climate Justice Action, for his lecture about the mobilization and press work for the COP 15, and to artist Ariel Schlesinger and designer Marco Carnevacci of Plastique Fantastique for sharing their specific knowledge on how to build inflatables. Susanne Quehenberger, a Berlin based student of cultural theory, gave a lecture on "Narratives in the Climate Change debate" and greatly influenced the organization of the workshop. A special thank-you goes out to Miriam Buyer, Via Campesina activist, for shipping the hammer in her regular traveling suitcase from Berlin to Mexico (without whose help, "El Martillo" would have been stuck at a Mexican post office).

The publication itself would never have come to fruition without the dedication of Kristin Gertz and Paul Pistorius, two Leipzig based graphic designers who spent more than half a year working on the making of the publication itself. At the very end of this, no doubt long introduction, we would also like to thank Alex Dunst for his generous help and for contributing with a text to this publication, Cristian Guerrero for all of his support, David Graeber for allowing us to publish excerpts from his excellent essay, and John Jordan and Isa Fremeaux of the "Laboratory of Insurrectionary Imagination", for being such an inspiration to us. A big thanks also to Alex Felicitas from Canada, who edited the final texts.

Jakub Simcik, Artúr van Balen
Eclectic Electric Collective

1 http://www.publications.parliament.uk/pa/cm200607/cmhansrd/cm070502/text/70502w0005.htm

2 This includes images of f.e. lonely polar bears on ice blocs, globes, CO2 bombs and windmills.

From: “Cristian Guerrero” <c.guerrero@riseup.net>
Subject: El Martillo is dead!
Date: Tue=2C 12 Dec 2010 12:24:06 -0500
To: “Artúr van Balen” <arturelectrico@gmail.com>

Hey you all,

I can’t express the regret and embarrassment I feel for what happened to the hammer, and for taking so long to contact you all after the COP 16 protests.
First off I must explain that my computer was stolen during the Cancún protest – apparently I was not the only one – many others lost equipment. I am just getting to be able to answer backdated email messages, since I had most of my messages and contacts on my computer. This has impacted us severely, due to the load of information I had on that particular computer – photos, docs, videos, etc… The good side is that many other folks have videos, photos, and many news articles where posted on the hammer and the protests.

The police and the hammer thing – I’m so sorry! The Anti-C@P protesters got a bit over-excited and hurtled it over the police-wall. I was not at the head of the march, and I think that everybody else assumed that that was what the hammer was for – smashing something. We didn’t have an actual plan at the time – we had in mind to at least take the hammer down to the police-wall for a picture or two… There was a general frustration in the air that day among many of the participants and protesters that the marches for climate justice on December 7th, called for by the Via Campesina and Climate Dialogue encampment organizers, refused to unite and march together. The Anti-C@P contingent, along with many others in the Via Campesina march also felt stifled to have been stopped by the march’s organizers blocks away from reaching the police-line that guarded the road to the COP16. Speech after tiring speech was given on the hot avenue asphalt for hours, and had scores of people scrambling for shade and for a better reason for being mobilized to march out there for several miles to fall a few blocks short from the seat of power we were there to protest. There was a sad sense of defeat that came from repeating the same-old routine of a long isolated march ending in never-ending grandiose speeches decrying the need for change.

At the very back-end of the march a group of us were busy preparing the hammer behind the Bus-Lee, while others were busy inviting people from the march to accompany us down to the police-line for the photo-shoot. As the rally of NGO speeches ended, and without a warning, a surge of energy from the hammer’s immense symbolism took ahold of the group of people carrying the hammer as they began shouting war-cries and yells, and then suddenly were off running toward the police-line chanting “A, A, Anti-COP!, A, A, Anti-COP!” with a horde of unsuspecting protesters and press-media rushing closely behind them. I came running behind them, wondering what had happened. As the bonsai-marathon-assault reached the security-wall, a battalion of a hundred riot-police guarding it from the front cleared out of the way as the group with the hammer in front crashed into the massive 3 meter metal security-wall that kept us from reaching the UN climate meetings. The hammer collided into the police-wall in a spectacular crash that released, at least momentarily, the indignation many of us were feeling of having to come so close to such a place of abuse of power and not being able to forcefully express not only our words, but also our will.

Since we received the hammer from Berlin, people here have had lots of fun trying to get it to stand straight-up, bouncing it up like a giant beach ball during the marches and practice drills at the encampments. Dozens of people would start jumping up at the same time hitting the hammer's head so that it would fly up and stand almost straight up on itself. After smashing into the police-wall the protesters started trying to do this and got the hammer to bounce high up and over the wall in a splendid smashing of the police-line positioned on the other side. Many cheered. But once the hammer was over the wall we had to get it back. I finally had made it up to the front of the protest and jumped up onto the security-wall with another friend and started pulling the hammer in a tug-of-war contest against the police who stubbornly gripped onto the hammer's head in desperate attempt to prevent more hammer smashing. Immediately I saw anti-riot cops on the other side of the wall pointing large caliber pellet shotguns at us. I quickly ducked down to yell at the press-media on our side of the fence to film or take pictures of the police with the shotguns – (the local newspapers the next day had a funny picture of us on the front-page yelling from up-top of the security-wall at the reporters below and pointing at the cops). Suddenly, a police commander on the other side of the wall gave the order and within seconds a riot-cop took out a large knife and began to cut the hammer's head off the handle that we had on our side of the wall. The hammer tore into two pieces as chants and yells from the dozens of protesters blasted the police for over-reacting and fearing a giant inflatable hammer-shaped balloon.

At that moment we sat down, surrounded by the mainstream and alternative press-media, and made a quick statement about the hammer and why we had come to Cancún. I'm sure you've seen the videos.

I'm not even sure if this message will make it out to you at all – the internet comes and goes were I am now in the jungles of Guerrero.

We'll be 100 % connected on-line in a few days – we can do the follow up meeting then?

We appreciate all the work you all have done. Many people here were left thrilled and impressed with the hammer and our work.

We must do it again sometime.

Cristian

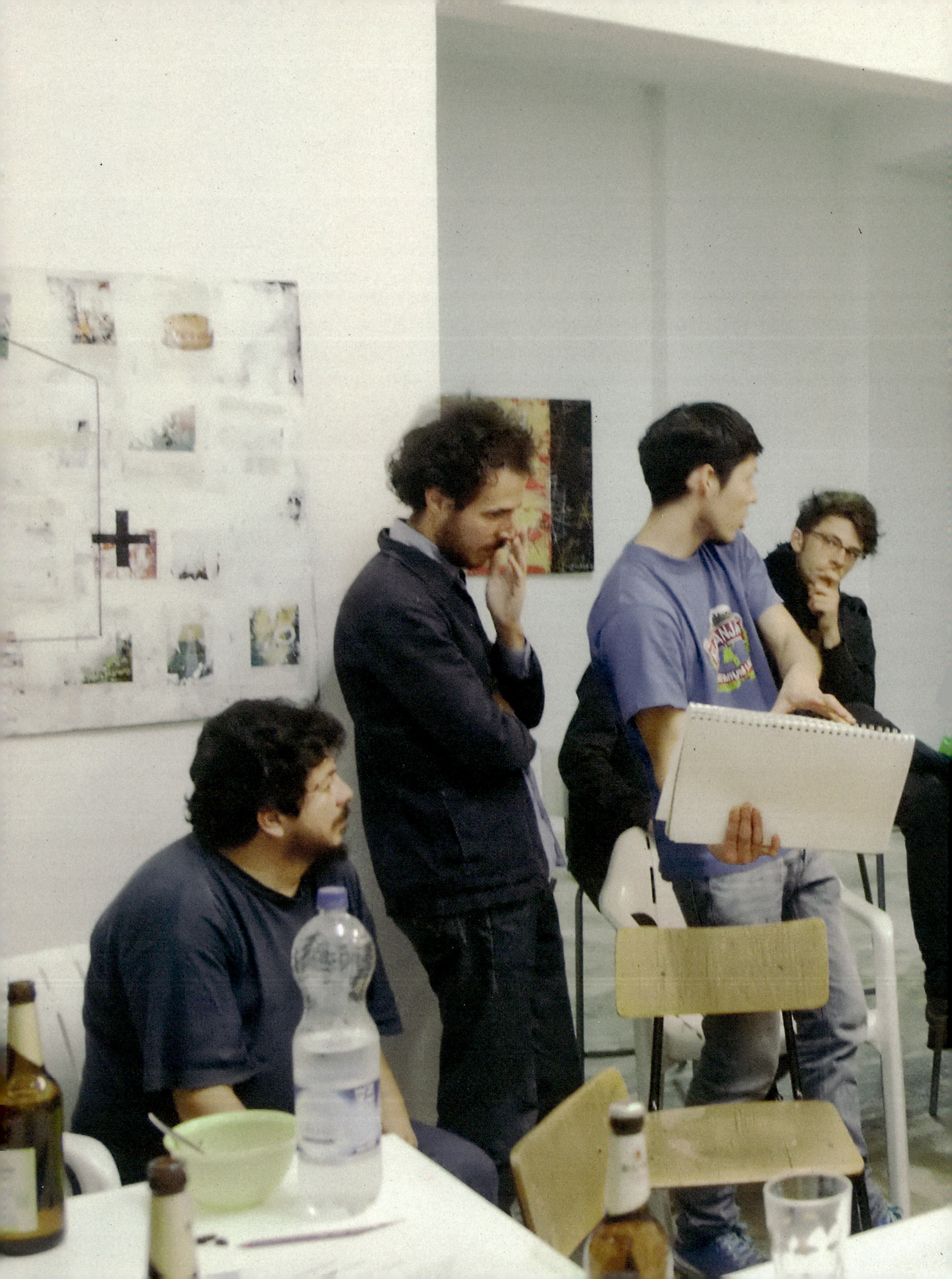

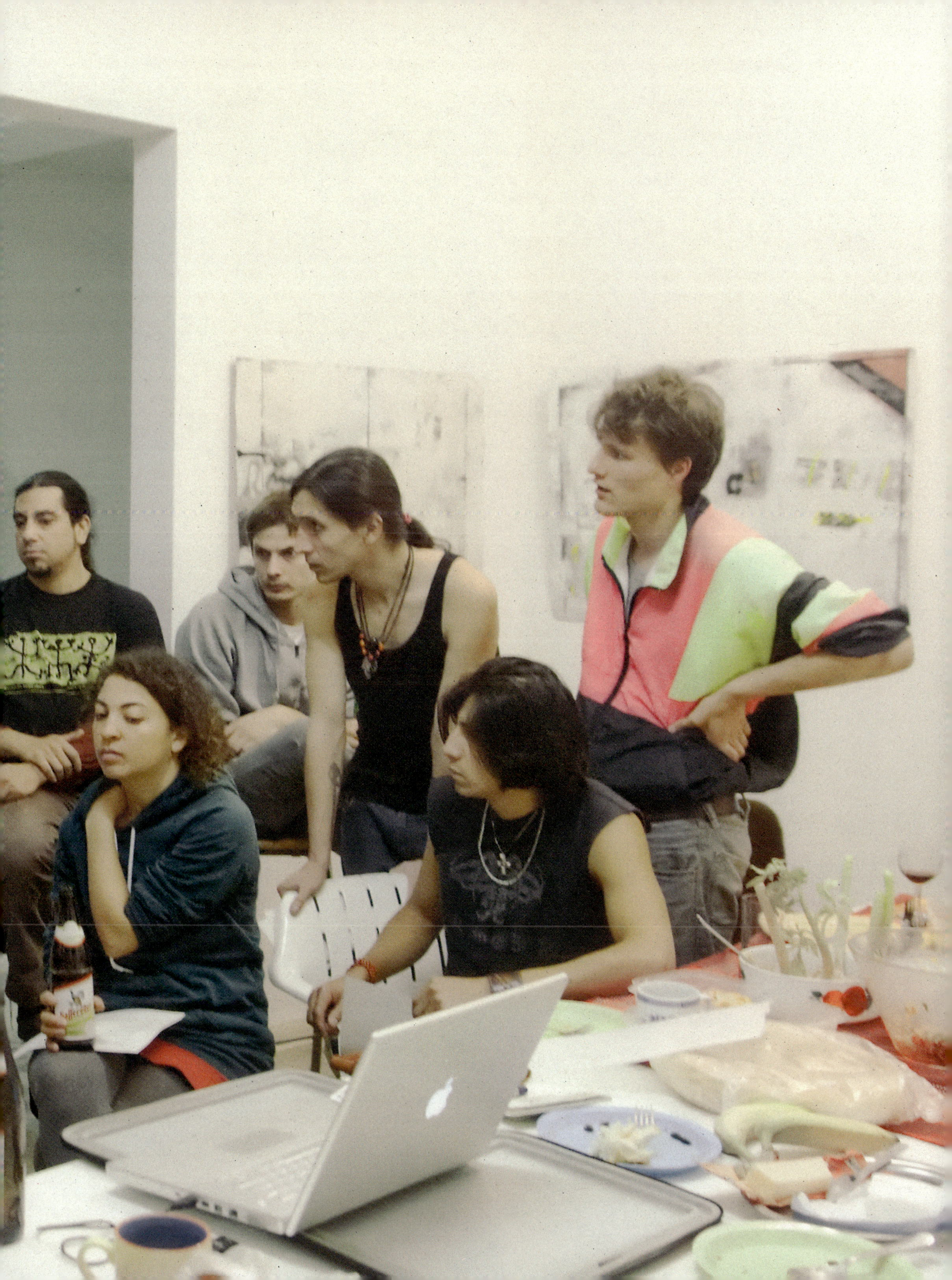

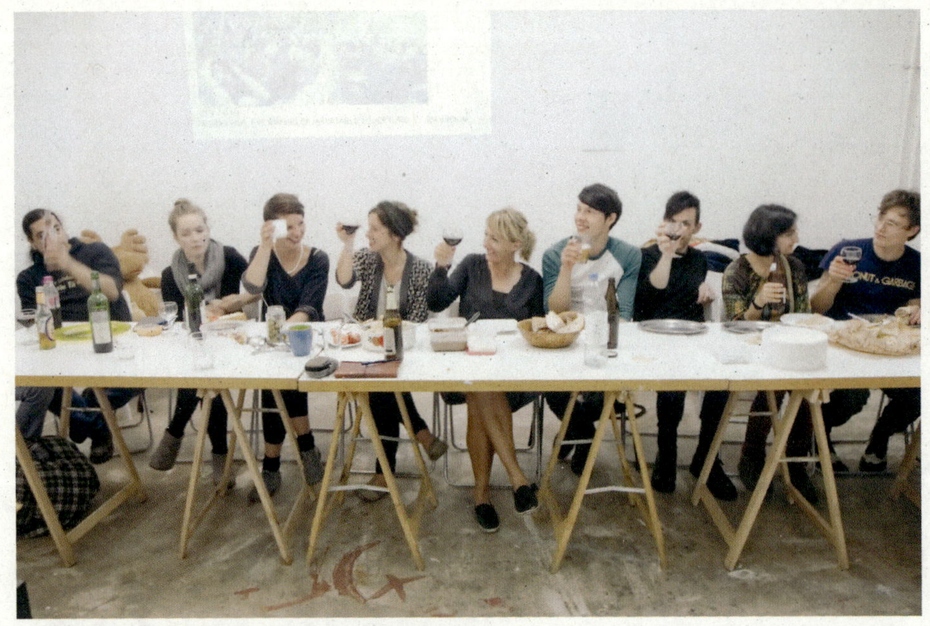
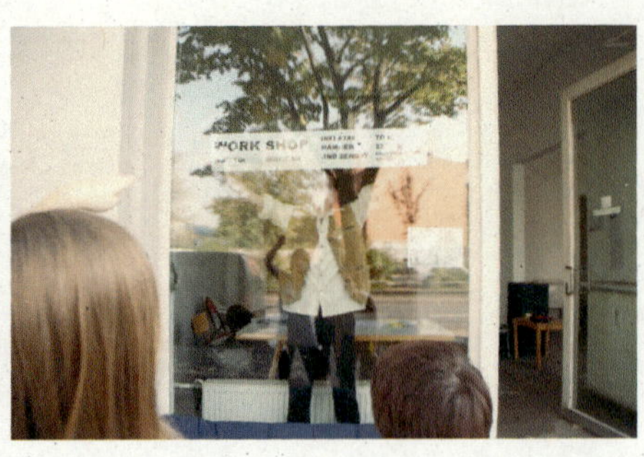
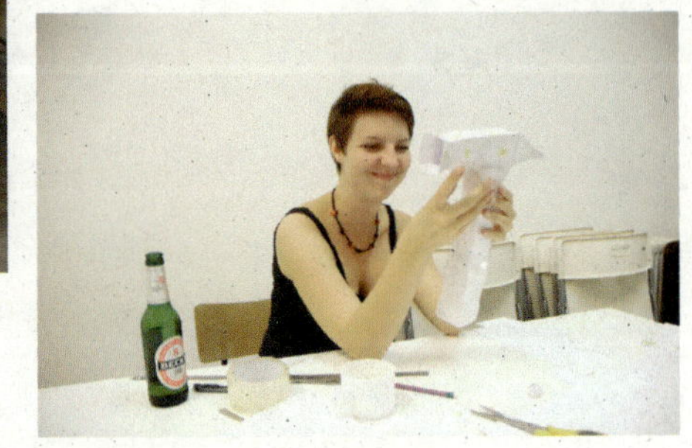
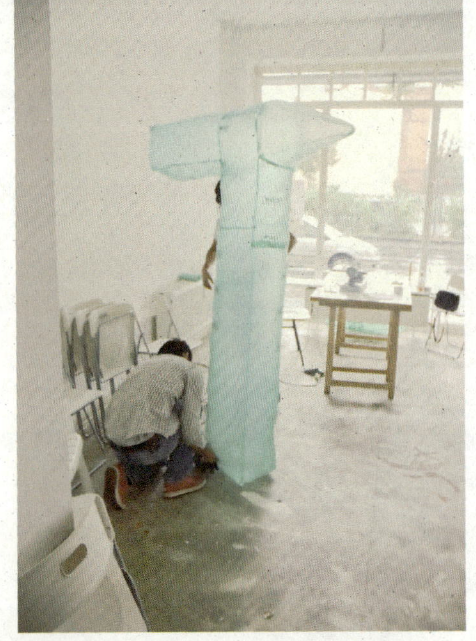
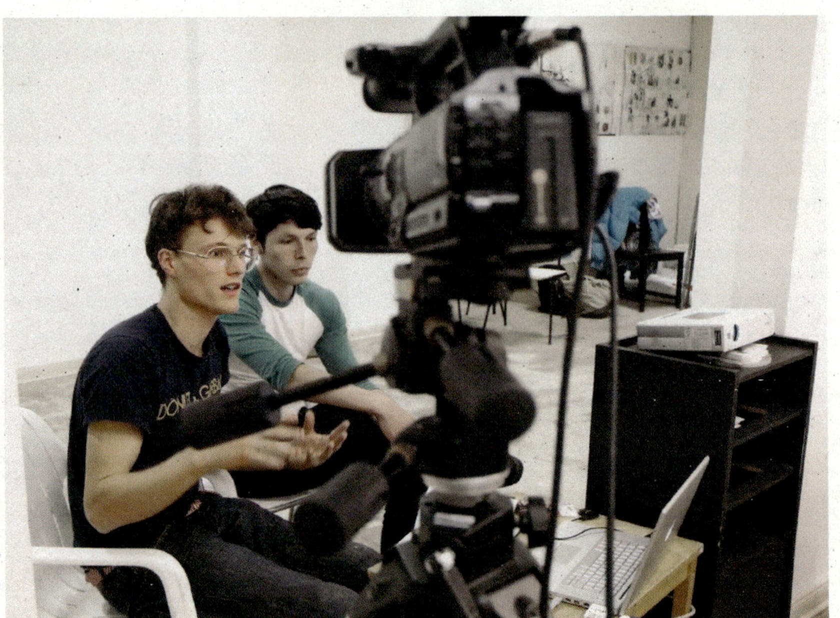
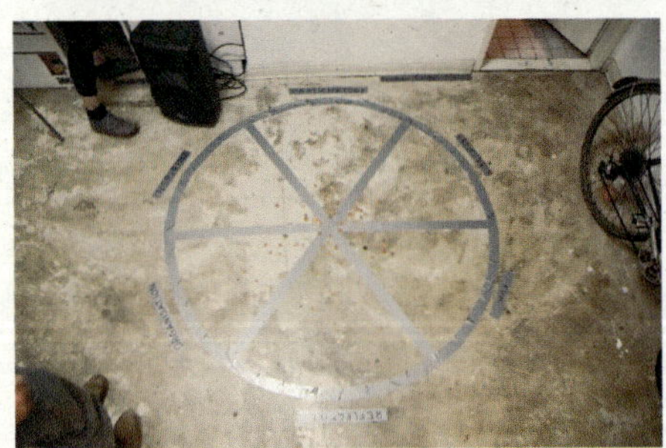
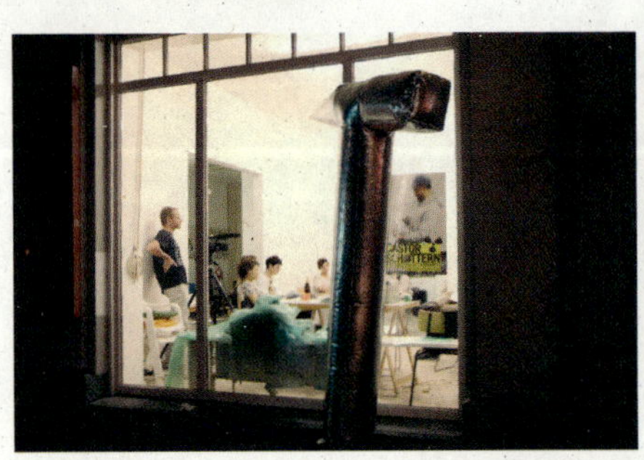
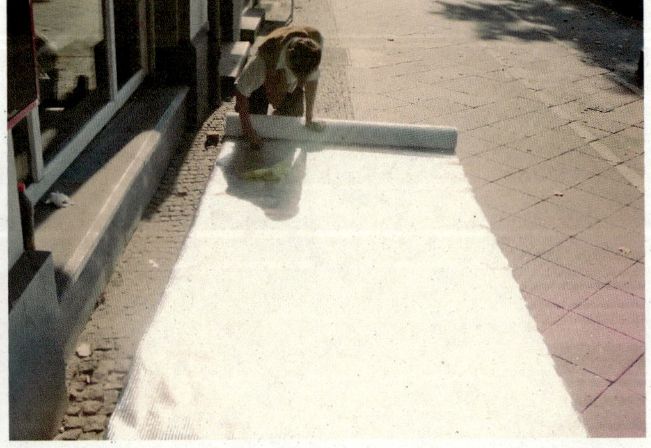

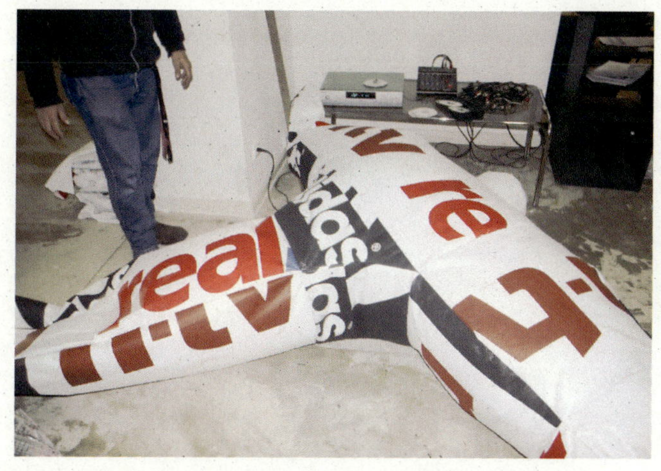
real

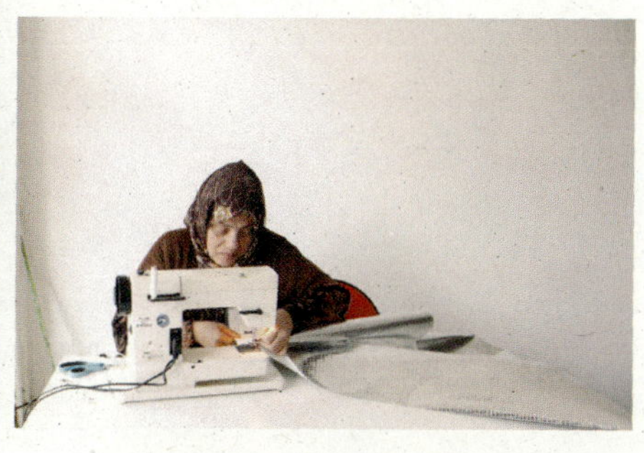

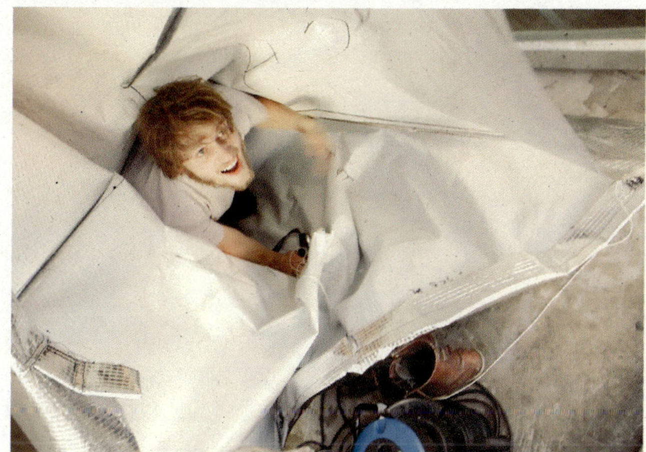

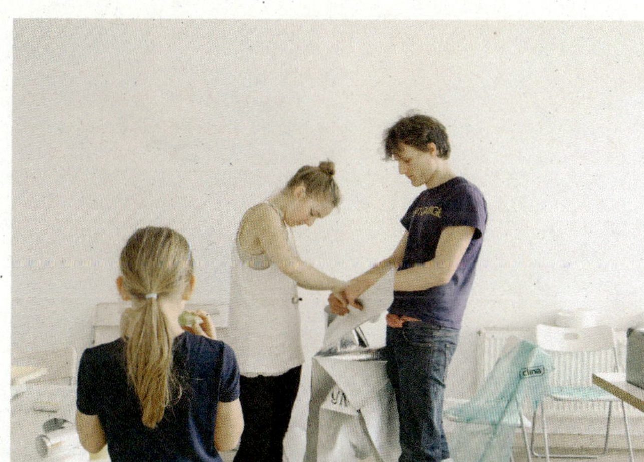

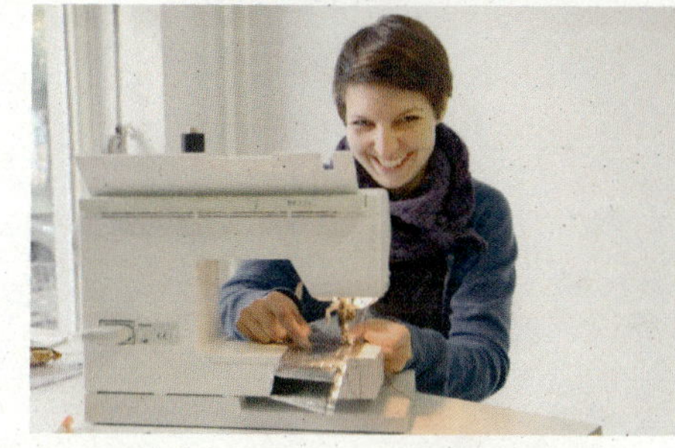

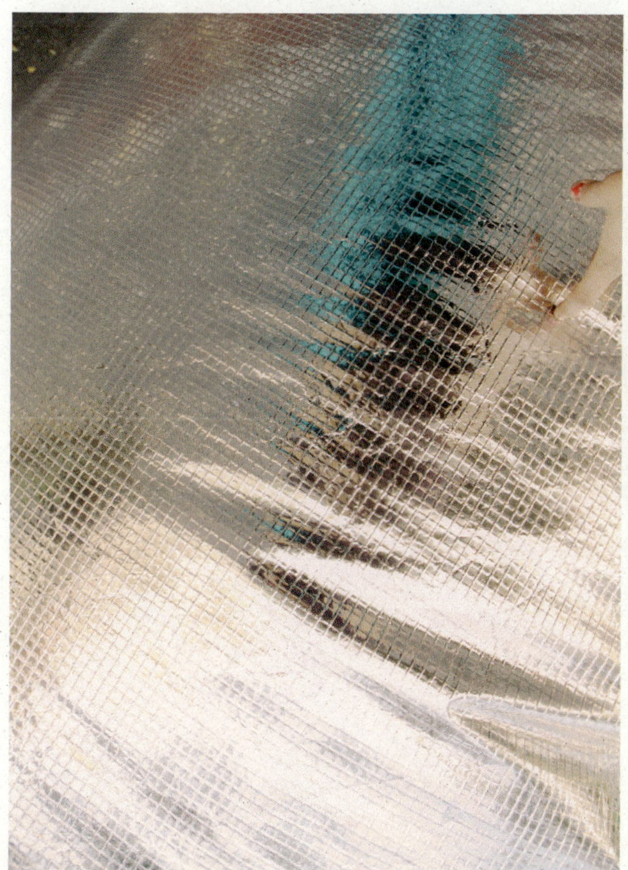

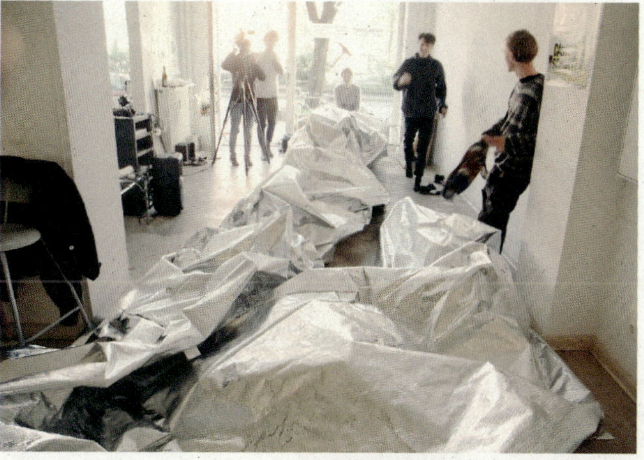

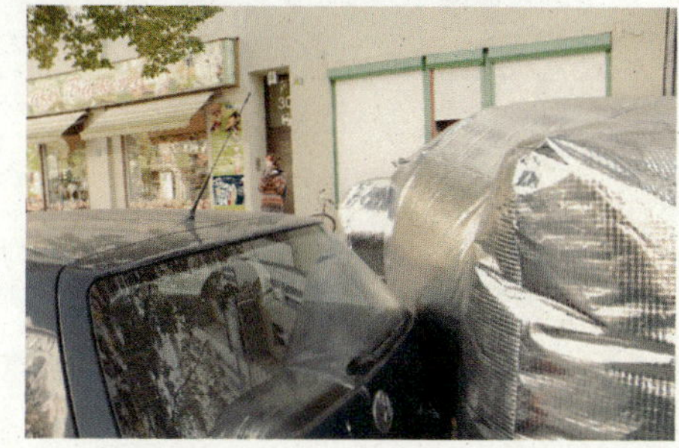

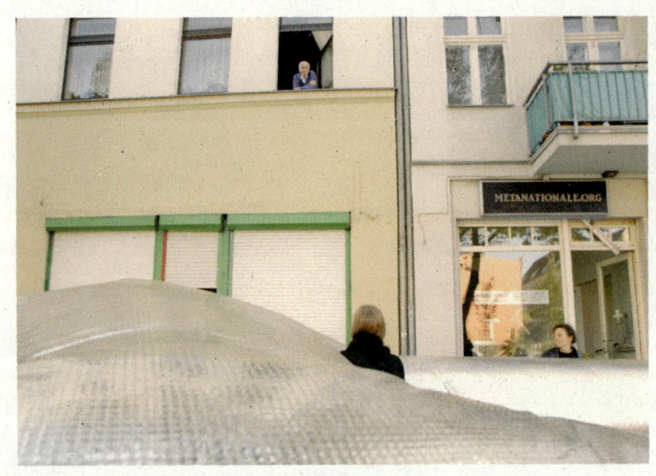
METANATIONALE.ORG

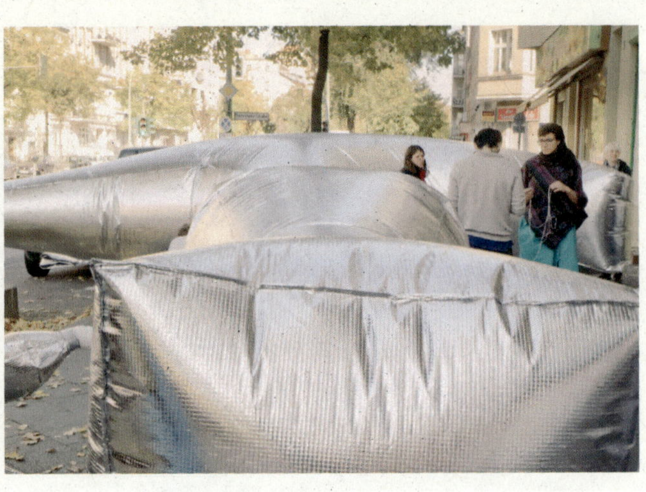

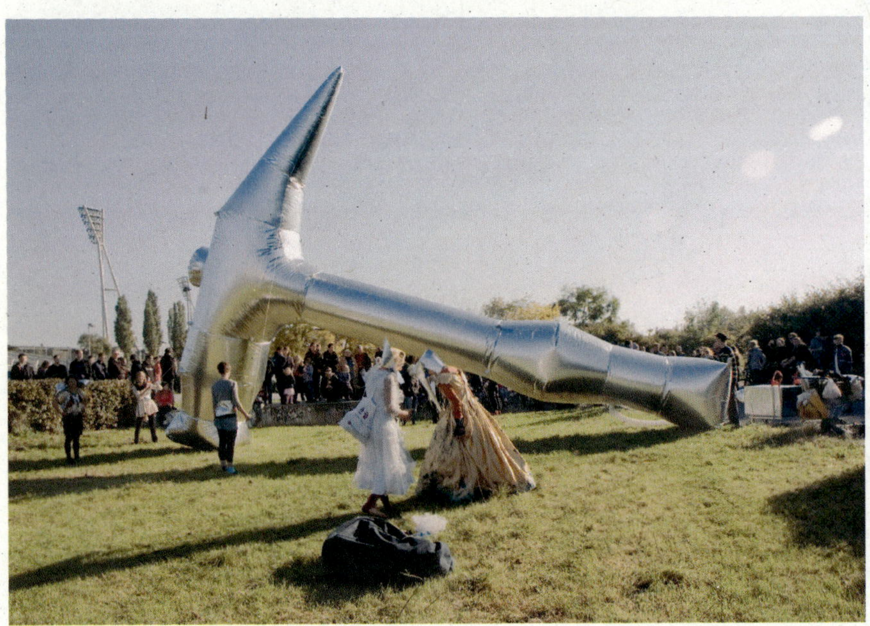

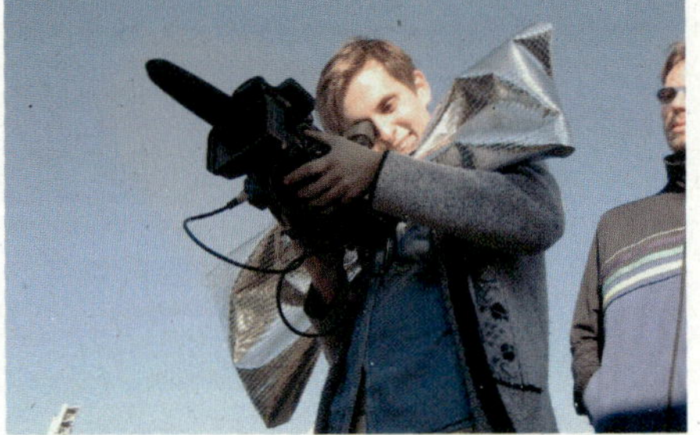

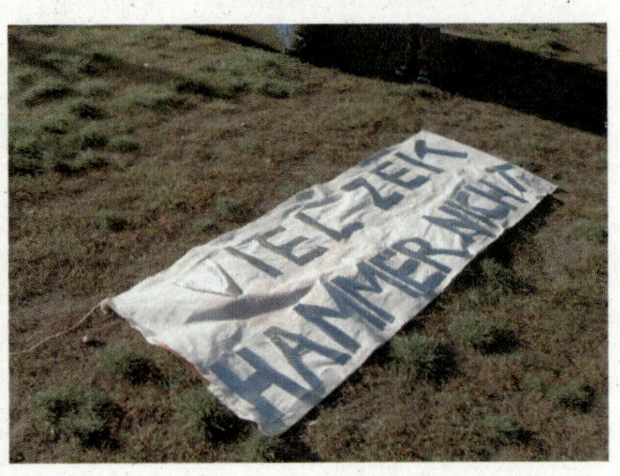
VIEL ZEIT
HAMMER NICHT

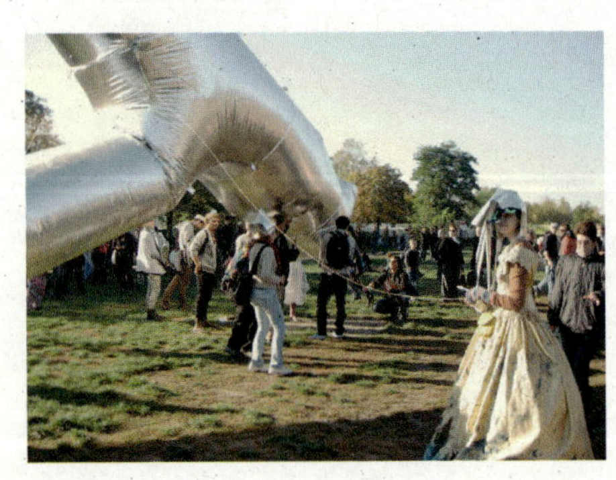

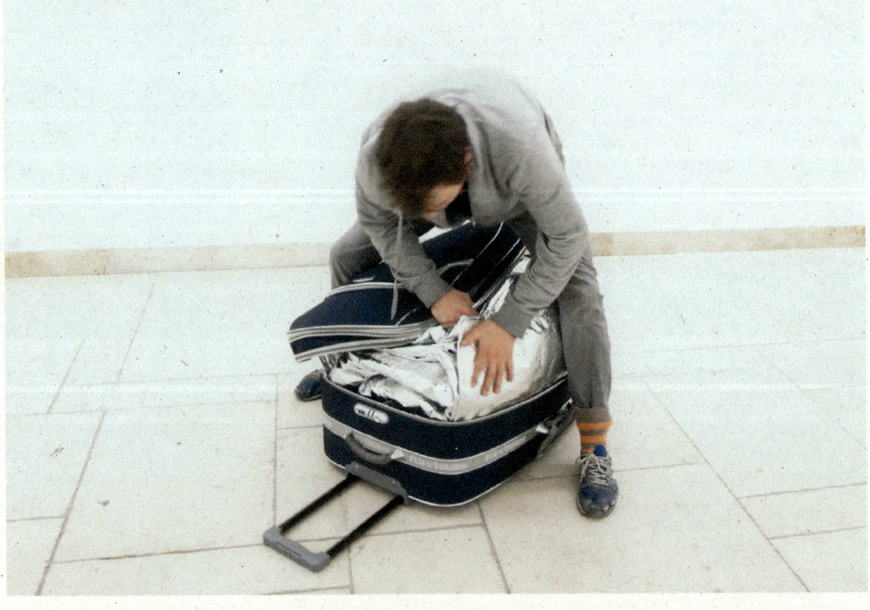

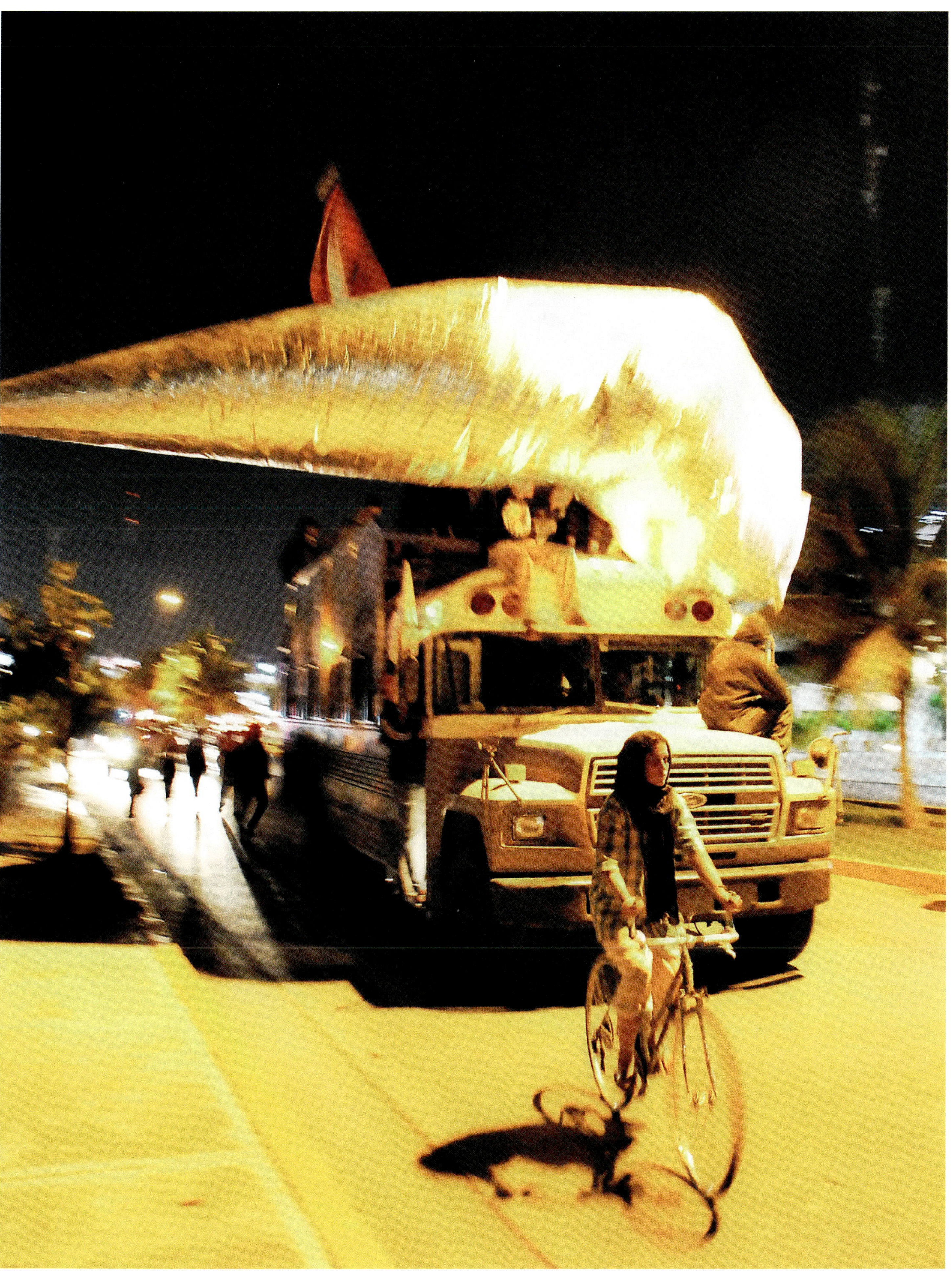

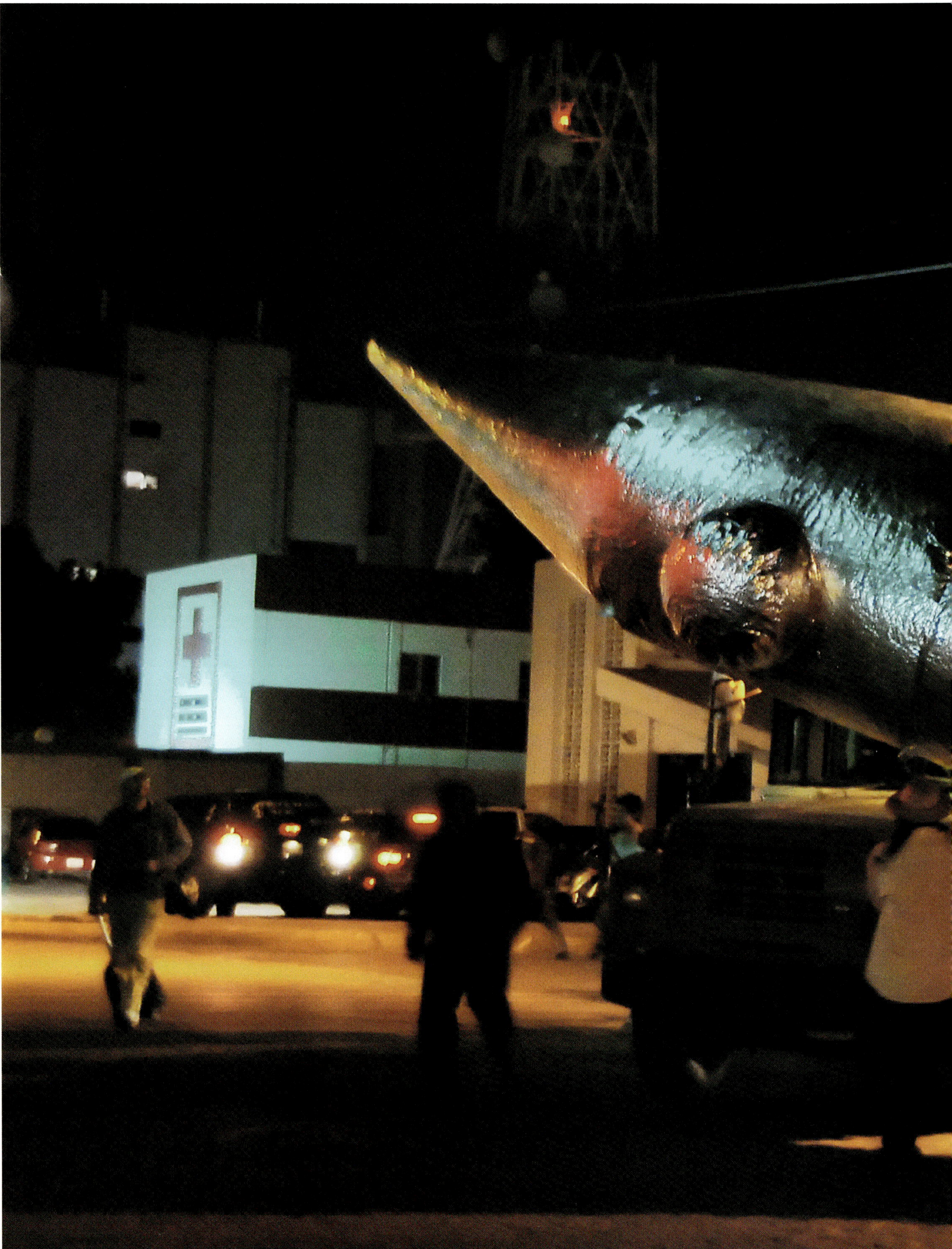

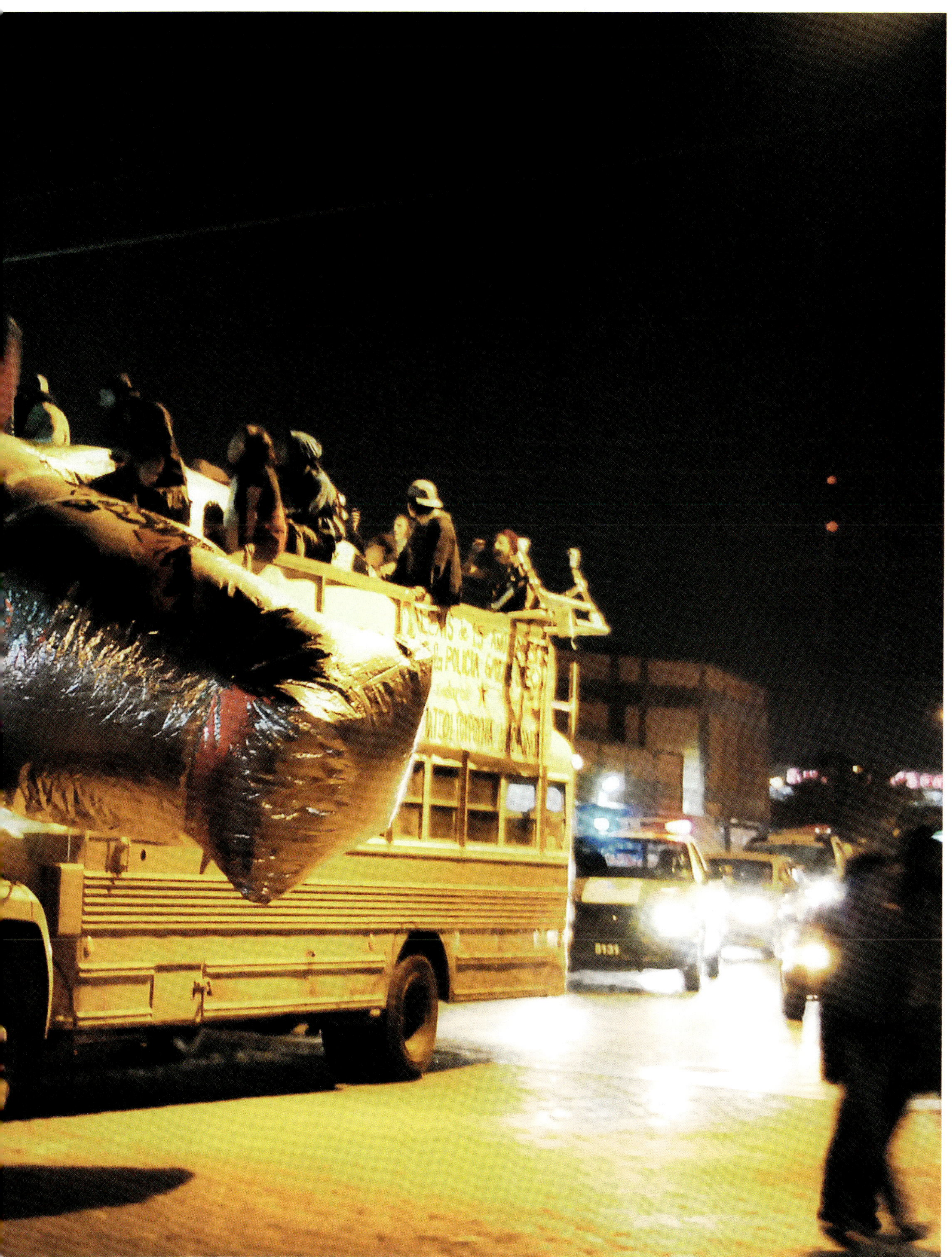

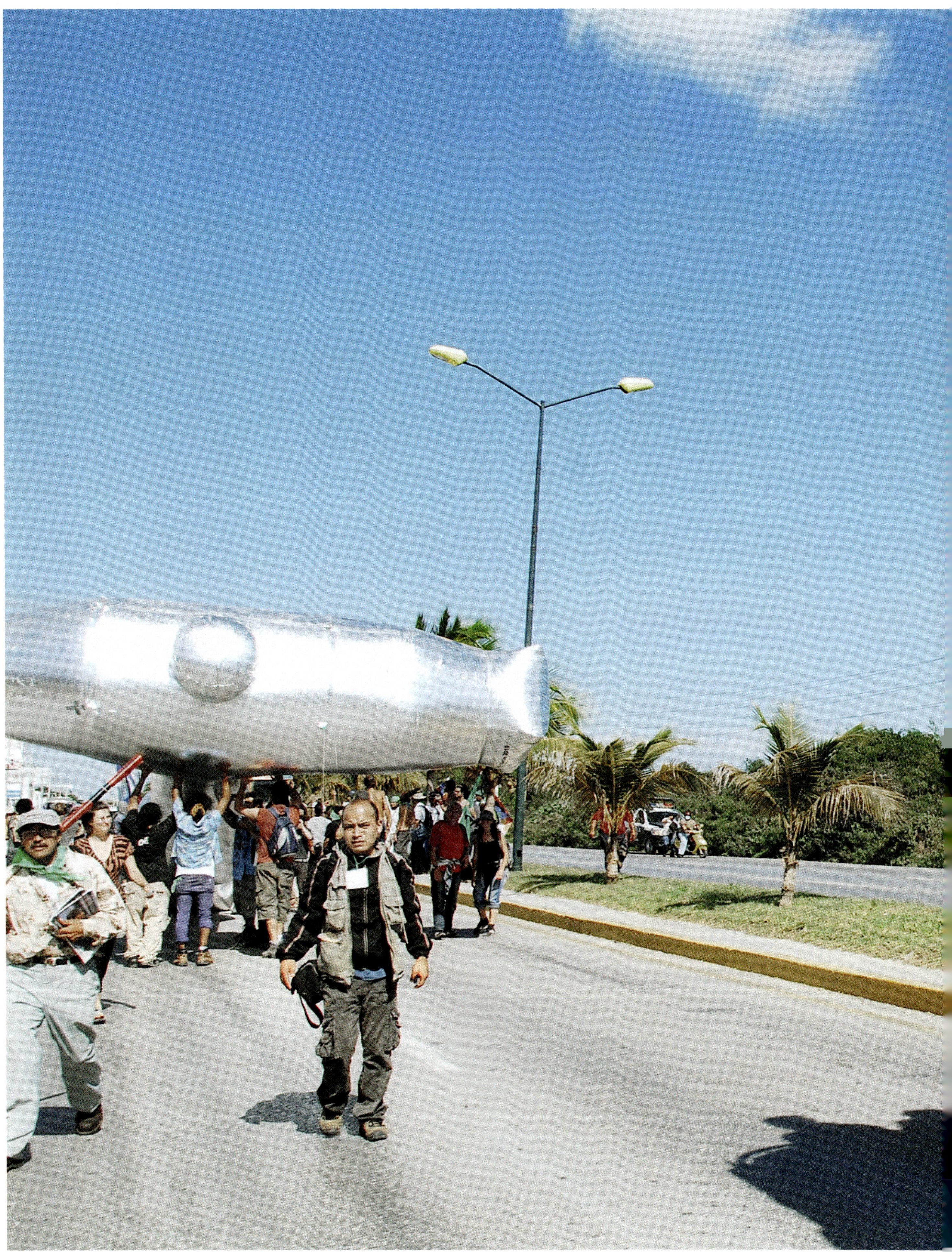

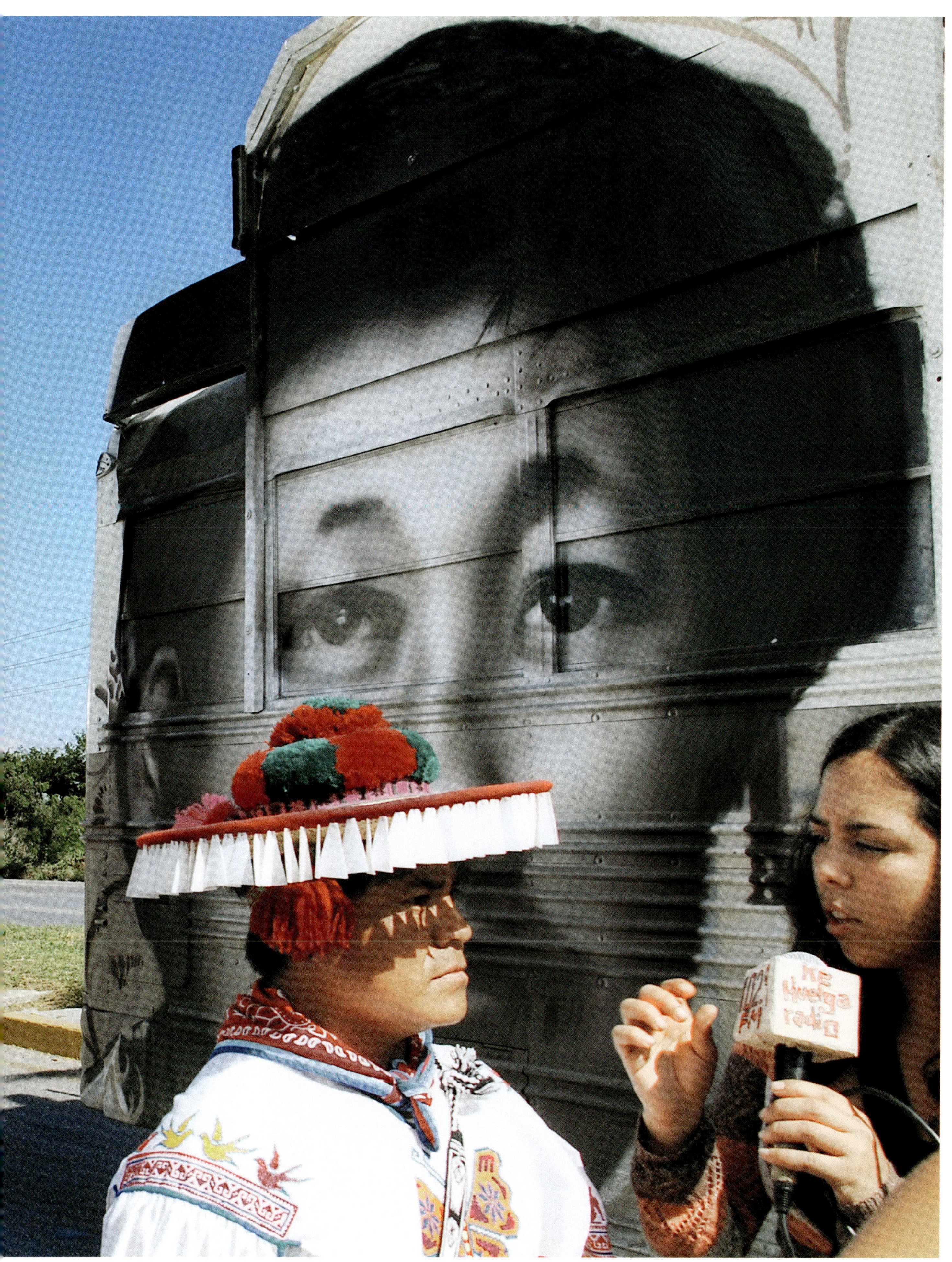
Ke
Huelga
radio

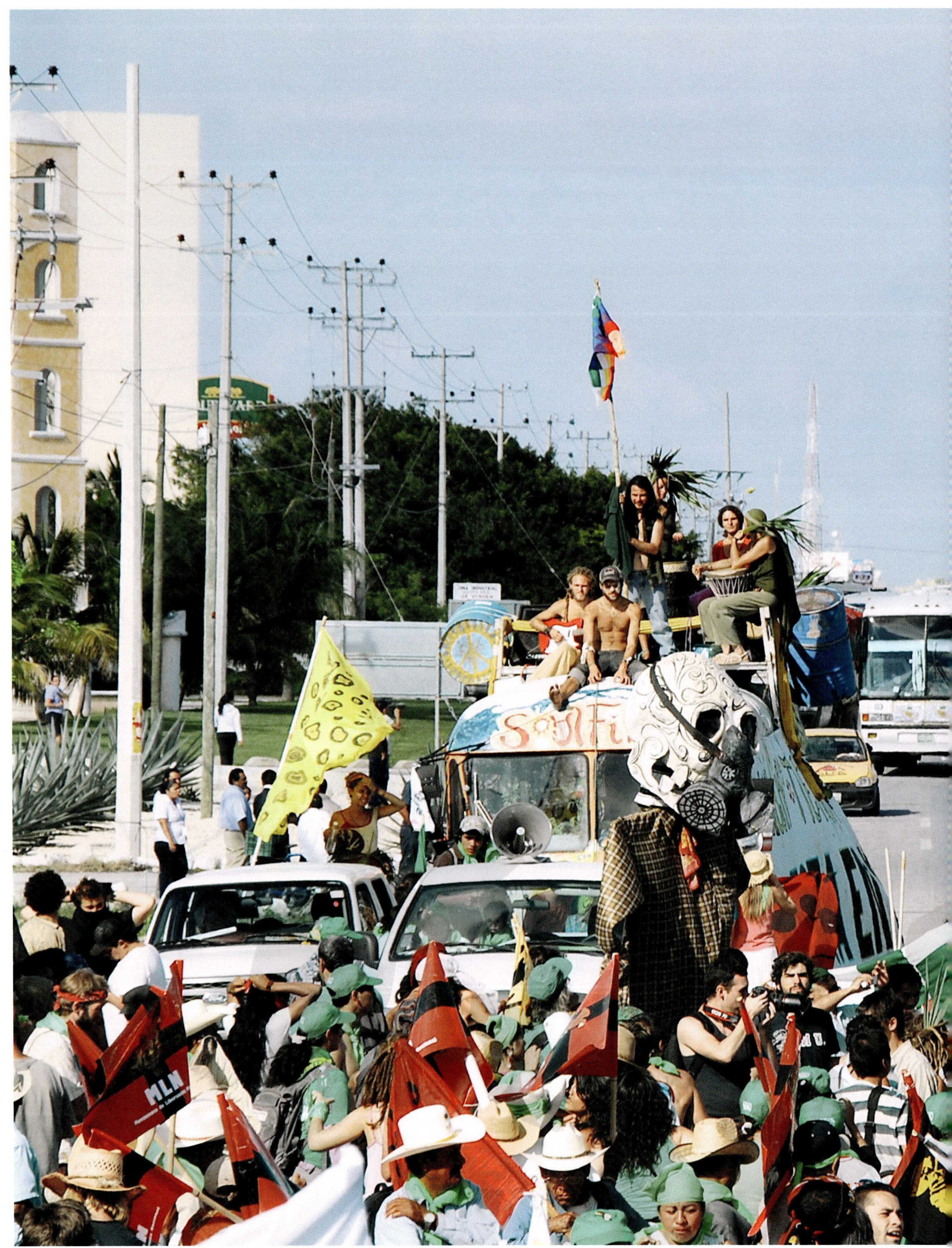
MLN

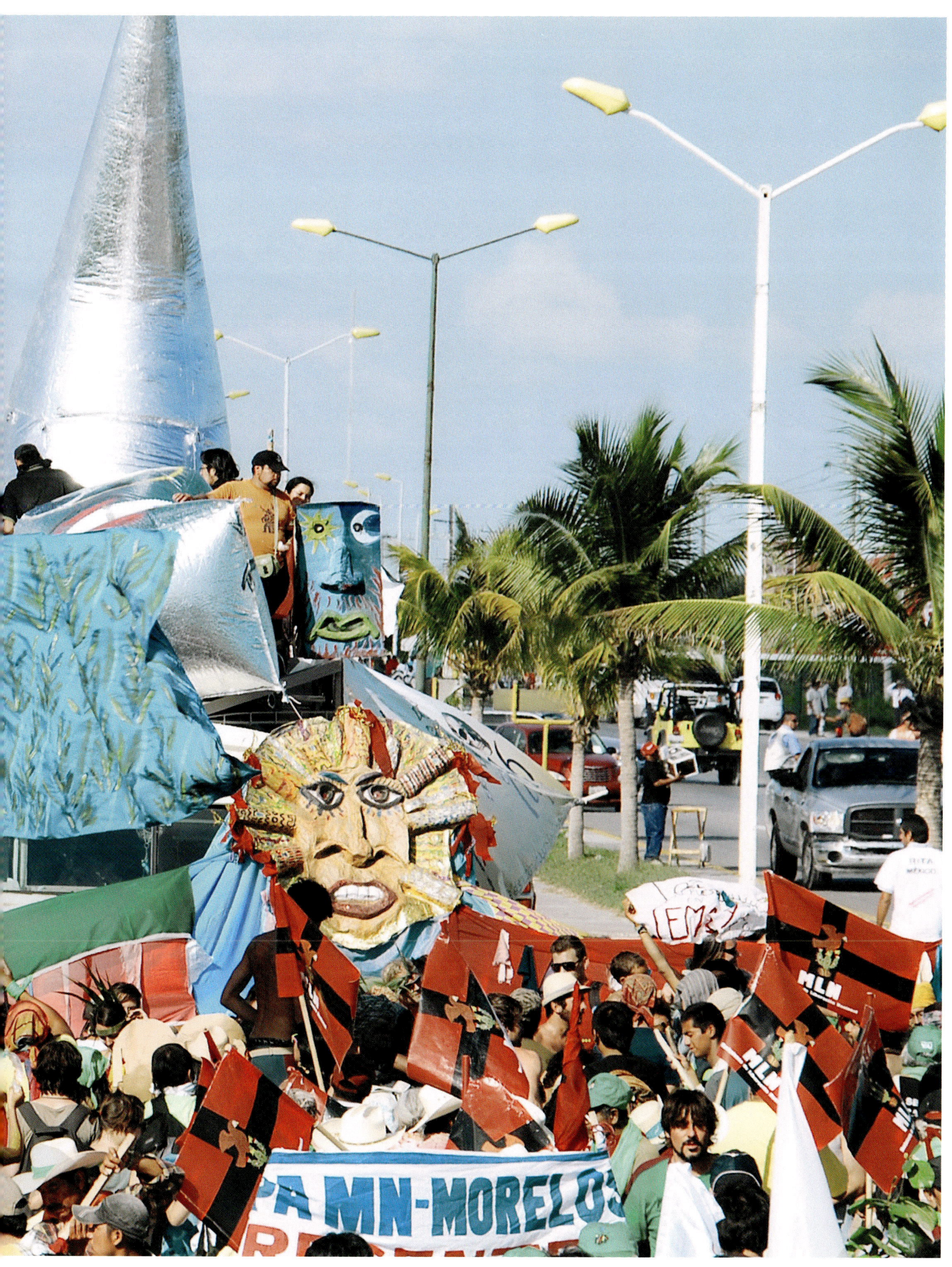
MLM
MLM
PA MN-MORELOS

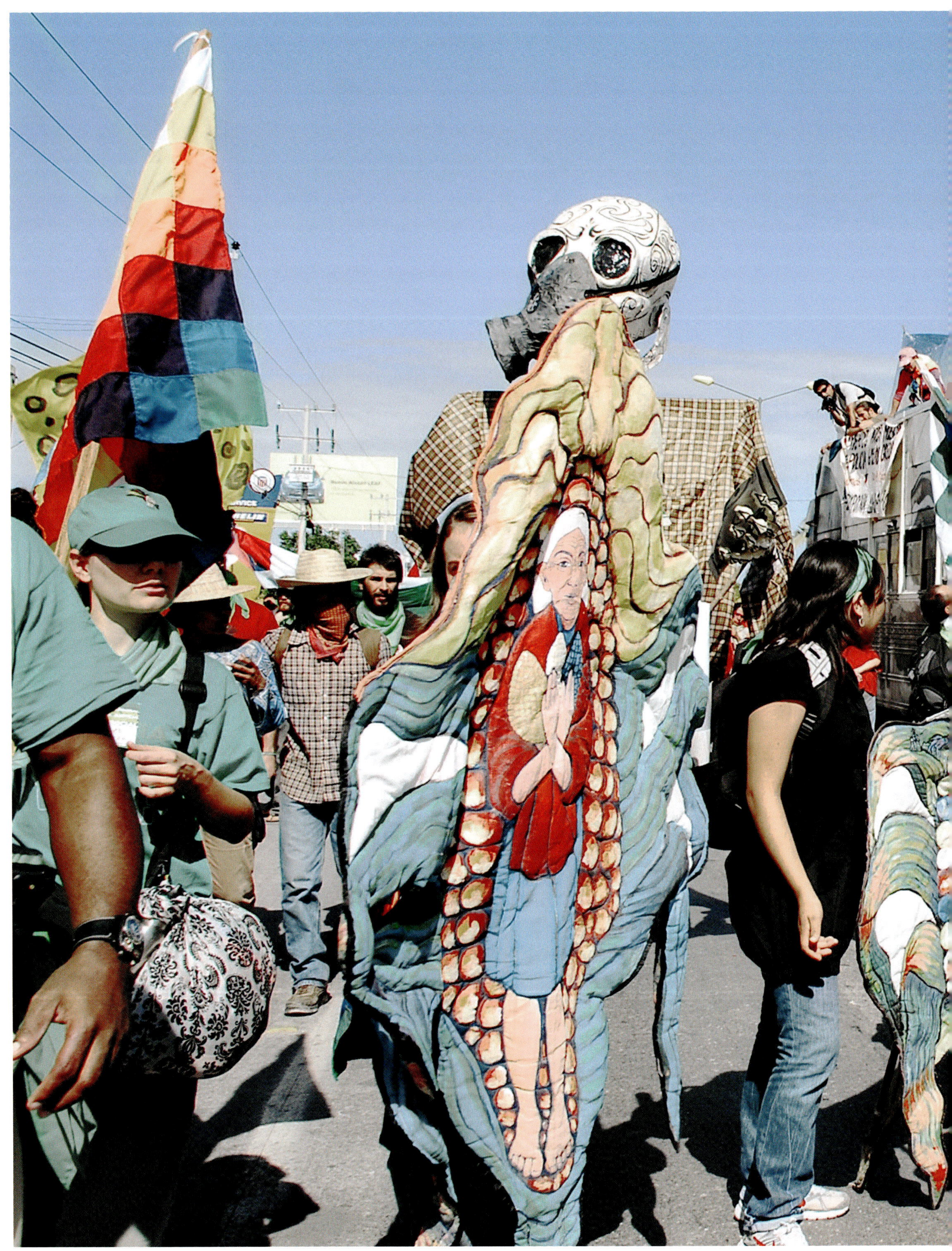

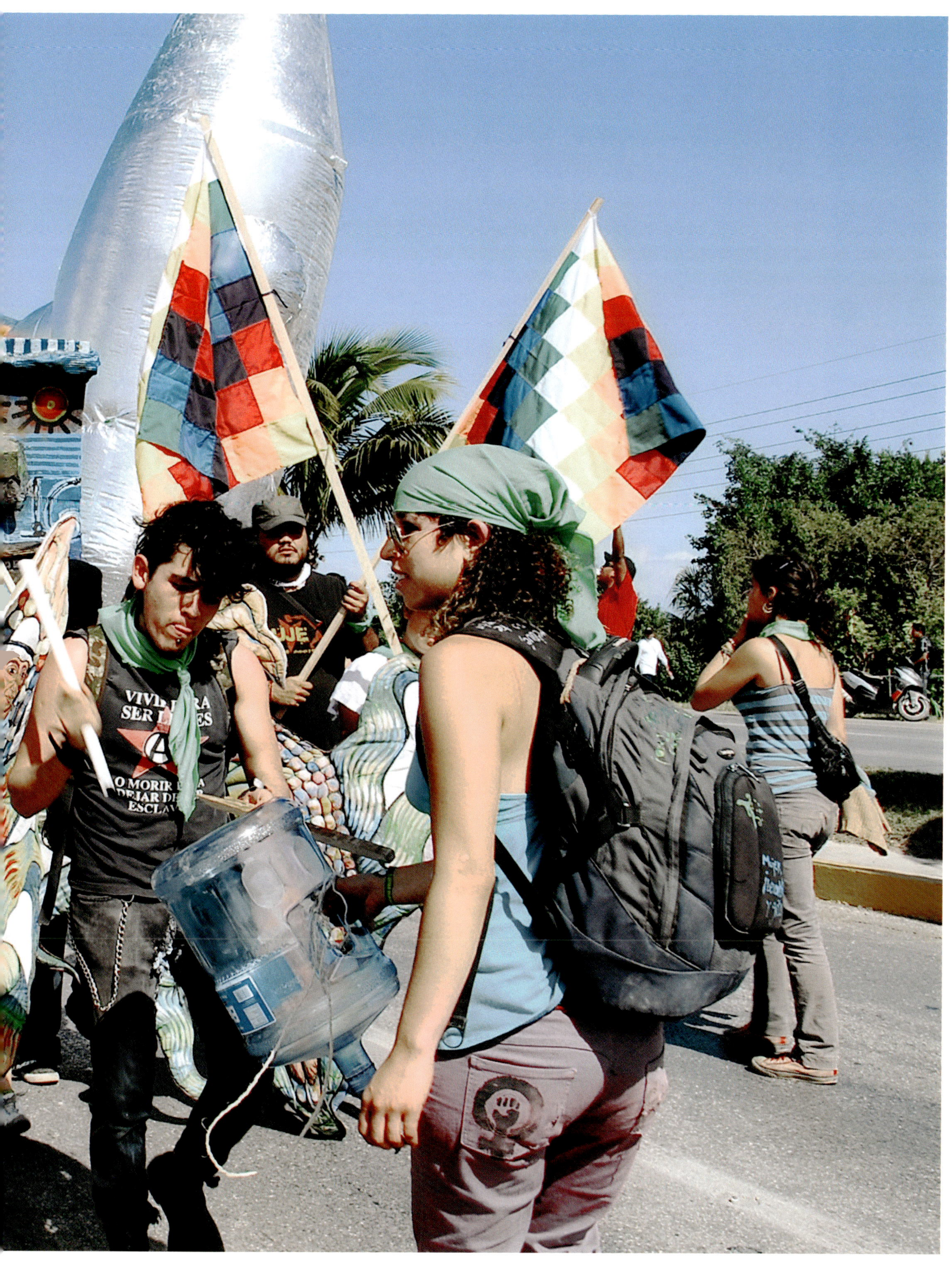

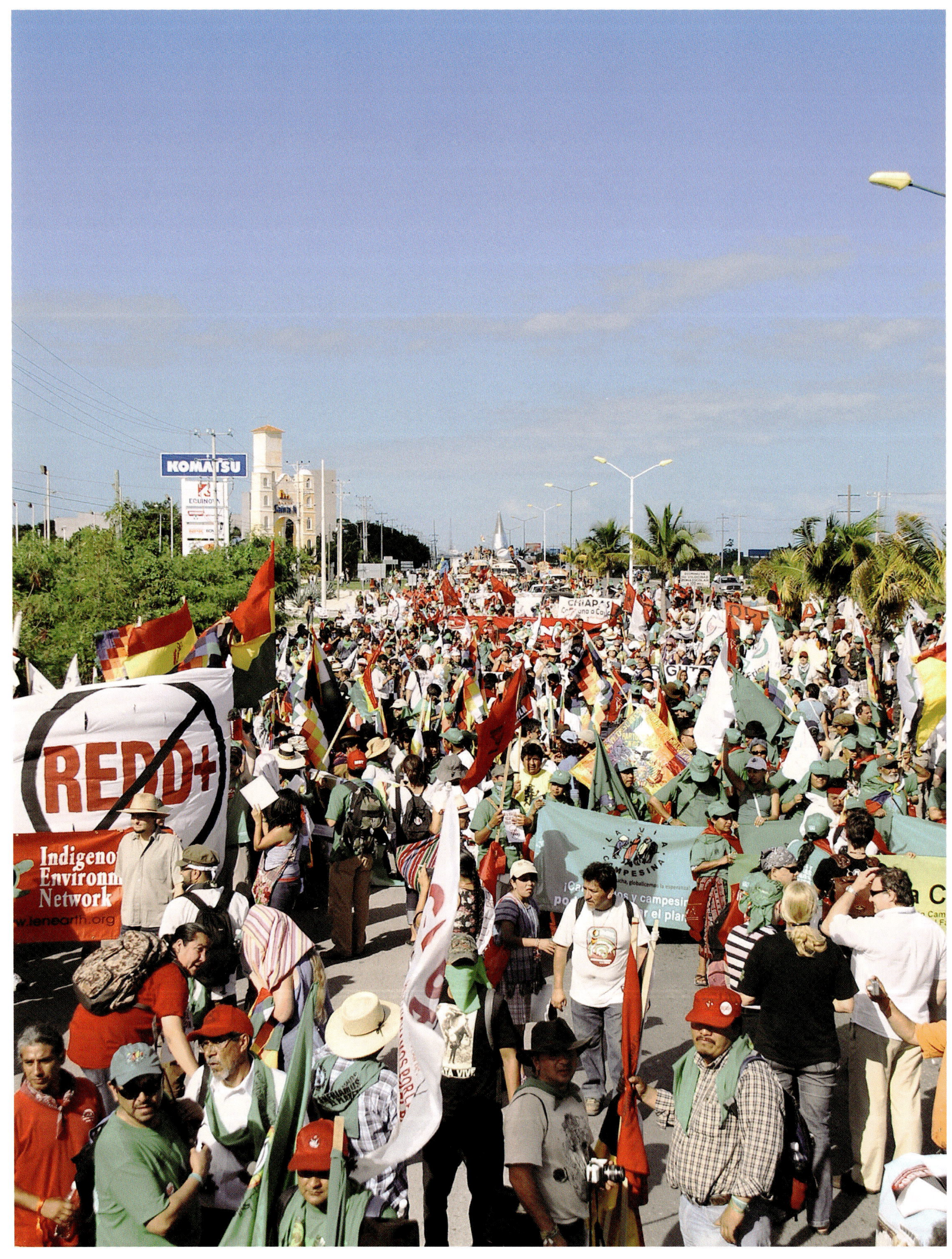
KOMATSU
REDD+
Indigeno
Environm
Network
ienearth.org
LA VIA CAMPESINA

Fighting for the Air we breathe

by Cristian Guerrero

In early spring of 2010, a number of us within Marea Creciente, the Mexican chapter of the international Rising Tide network, began making preparations for the COP 16 climate summit, taking place in Cancún later that year. As a diverse network of climate activists, scientists, and campaigns spread across four continents, Marea Creciente is dedicated to "confronting the root causes of the climate crisis"[1] – the institutions, policies, and industries that endanger communities and the natural environment.

Becoming host country to a UN Conference of the Parties meeting challenged our national climate justice network to respond in a creative and direct manner, organizing with other independent activists and collectives around the country a dynamic grassroots outreach, education, and mobilization campaign. This multi-faceted project was aimed at networking with local struggles and social organizations around the world to stimulate a mass mobilization towards the COP 16 meeting, but confronting at the same time the Mexican government's public-relations campaign to pass-off various controversial regional development projects and national climate policies as sustainable *clean development* initiatives within the spotlight of presiding over the United Nation's Framework Convention on Climate Change (UNFCC).[2]

Throughout the year before the COP 16 summit, we collaborated with a number of community groups and collectives and organized local workshop-events and regional gatherings around the country – we called these gatherings the "Regional Climate Convergences". The first convergence was held in April in Oaxaca City, and was dubbed the "Gathering for Autonomous Living". The second installment took place in August at the Biosphere Reserve Tehuacan-Cuicatlan, in the state of Puebla, and the third in October in San Salvador de Atenco, in the state of Mexico: bastion of the renowned "Peoples Front in Defense of the Land". There were also two bi-national convergences that took place in November close to both of the borders of the country: in Mexicali, in the state of North Baja California, and in San Cristobal de las Casas, Chiapas, in Zapatista territory.

Each one of these "climate camps" drew together various experiences of struggles for ancestral territories, environmental defense, and of displacement and immigration in the region. They brought together local and regional campaigns and people from neighboring states with the aim to form and articulate demands and action strategies of resistance towards a growing number of developing infrastructure mega-projects in Mexico – in particular open-pit mines and large-scale dams. These convergences also went further in formulating proposals for autonomous community solutions to the climate crisis that were shared and reflected on between each gathering.

As a collective process of construction these convergences also served to establish the working relationships that gave birth to the mobilization efforts towards the COP 16 climate summit that we were primarily involved in: the *International AntiC@P Space*. The "AntiC@P" for short, was nurtured within the context of shared social struggles in Mexico – it was born from individuals sharing political affinities and years of experience working together within many other grassroots campaigns, and with a common understanding of the underlying nature and cause of the current climate crisis.

We believe that *capitalism* is at the heart of this great and disastrous phenomenon that we all face. In our dire relationship as modern society with the Earth, it is this prevailing economic paradigm that consistently obligates and maintains societies and its governing institutions to value monetary profits over the well-being of its communities and natural eco-systems. We believe it is necessary to interpret it in this way in spite of the criticism from many within the climate justice movement, who feel that openly renouncing capitalism alienates people from joining the movement. Nonetheless, our analysis and resolve is invariably – anti-capitalist, or, "Anticap".

Declaring oneself "AntiCOP", however, can be even more uncomfortable for some – we realize it's not a side that many are ready to take – that of abandoning this process, and even going as far as being against it. Even so, we feel it necessary to draw a line in the sand, so to speak; to create a boundary to respect fundamental differences in our beliefs: Between those who believe that a corrupted treaty born from the UN COP process can effect essential and positive structural changes in "modern" industrial capitalist society's daily patterns of producing and consuming – and those who consider this method to be not only an unfortunate waste of time and valuable resources in the name of the people of the world, but also a plain-view hi-jacking of the struggle for climate justice.

Built upon the awareness that we had gained about the COP process and all of its misgivings through the campaigning, publications, and the collective learning we stimulated during these climate convergences, the AntiC@P initiative only had one true goal: to stand in clear opposition to the wholesale selling-off of our Mother Earth through this international treaty that would legalize the right to pollute the air we breathe; thereby creating a whole new market economy out of all that is natural and wild. The COP process and the UNFCCC is what Tom B.K. Goldtooth, director of the IEN, calls the "WTO of the Sky".[3]

A GIFT FROM THE OTHER SIDE OF THE ATLANTIC

Around mid-summer the Eclectic Electric Collective from Berlin sent a message over one of the email list serves that had been used for promoting the COP16 mobilizations. They asked if anyone had any information on groups or artist collectives who might be organizing protests and mobilizations activities towards the COP16. The collective proposed to send a giant inflatable *thing* to Mexico, as a visual prop for the marches and direct actions which were expected to happen before and during the climate summit. We struck a chord with our new made friends in Germany, and we began to hash out a plan to ship this mysterious inflatable thing from Europe to Mexico: What was to become a collective expression of symbolism and action as an inspiring message to those paying attention to the failing UN climate "negotiations" as they unfolded.

A powerful sense of excitement came over us when our friends from Eclectic Electric Collective told us that the inflatable "thing" being sent from Europe was going to be a giant hammer – a 12-meter tall, silver protest-hammer. The collective had even put together a very special online users-manual video to explain how to inflate the giant tool.

The newly formed AntiC@P mobilization took to the task using the hammer for the first time during a well-attended protest march in Mexico City on November 19th – "National Day of Repudiation of the Bad Government" – and one day before the bicentennial anniversary of the Mexican Revolution. We suffered only minor battle-scars during this first exhibition exercise, due to puncture holes in the hammer from tree branches and traffic posts along the march's route.

We were better prepared for the second "hammer-time" in Mexico City, during the "Day of Action for Climate Justice" on November 30th – start date of the official climate summit in Cancún. In a heated mobilization with tens of thousands of people in the street, the protest-hammer was inflated atop our *protest-bus*, and towered along side Mexico City's financial district's skyscrapers as the march moved down Reforma Avenue. We nicknamed the remodeled school bus "Bus-Lee", after the Korean small-farmer leader and activist Lee Kyung-Hae who died immolated during the WTO protests of 2003, also in Cancún.[4]

The bus was painted over with a mural dedicated to his memory, and to honor the international anti-globalization movement that defeated the World Trade Organization that year.

This action was the kick-off to the Via Campesina caravan "For Life, Social, and Environmental Justice" to the COP16 in Cancún – a three day marathon of rally-stops in communities represented in the National Assembly of the Environmentally Harmed.[5] Though the time-sensitive nature of this caravan provided us with little opportunity to inflate and display the hammer along the way.

Once in Cancún, the AntiC@P numbers swelled into the hundreds with people arriving on other caravans from other states and countries. We organized the "International AntiC@P Space" on one of the baseball fields in the large sporting complex Jacinto Canek that the Via Campesina had obtained just in time for arrival of the mass mobilizations and caravans. The idea was to create an autonomous open forum and program with workshops, video-screenings, assembly and meeting spaces; and an area for working on direct-action props: banners, giant puppets, and all things inflatable.

In the first days of the AntiC@P space, during one of the open assemblies organized in the evenings, a protest "against green-capitalism" was proposed and agreed upon for December 6th. Feeding off a sense of desire from the hundreds of protesters that gathered in Cancún to cause a little ruckus during the official climate proceedings, this "night-action" was organized to target the local PROFEPA offices,[6] the primary governmental agency in Cancún charged with facilitating the privatization of beaches and costal properties considered to be public domain.

Returning back to the AntiC@P encampment space, we took advantage of the branch-less palm trees that lined the wide avenues of downtown Cancún, to unfurl the inflatable giant atop of the Bus-Lee for an evening exhibition of the protest-hammer. Locales and tourists gawked in awe as they watched the shimmering colossal roll slowly by, reflecting back the city lights and photo-camera flashes. Waves and whistles were received as if the people in the street were greeting a well-known celebrity.

The next day on December 7th, thousands of people assembled out onto the hot Caribbean avenue for the Via Campesina march, and it was said that tens of thousands more in solidarity protests around the world answering the call to action to create "1000 Cancúns". The hammer came raised in full glory shining in the afternoon sun as we now came following the march from behind. Some of the most memorable and reproduced pictures of that day by the media have the hammer standing behind the thousands of protesters coming down the long avenue.

At one point as we gradually moved down the avenue the dozens of people encircling the bus started to play with the hammer like a giant beach ball, bringing it down off the top of the bus and bouncing it up in the air trying to get the hammer to stand straight up on itself. This turned into quite a scene, as dozens more people joined into this synchronized collective jumping and bouncing of the hammer, watching it fly higher and higher up with each jumping push.

Suddenly, the organizers of the march had decided to stop the procession a half-kilometer away from the police wall that blocked our path to the COP 16 convention centers. As the organizers decided to end their impromptu rally and return back to their camping space, a burst of screams and chants started to yell out from the crowd of people playing with the hammer. Within moments this group went racing by with the hammer hoisted above their heads running down the avenue towards the police wall as if they were convinced they were carrying a huge battering ram!

The hammer had been partly thrown over the police wall and within seconds was decapitated by the riot cops on the other side. A sense of rage and discouragement came over the crowd of protesters as they began kicking and banging on the metal police barricade. But in an act of vindication, we collectively came together in front of the police-wall, sat calmly down onto the street pavement, and gave a short statement to the press media assembled there around us.

Reporters and journalist kept repeating the questions "Who are you?", "What is your name?", to which we answered again and again, the "International AntiC@P Space".

Our visual prop had exceeded its expectations, as it merged beautifully with the allegory we were playing out as the *AntiC@P block* – that of smashing out the institutions of the past that have defrauded and failed us for so long in this struggle for climate justice; and at the same time, that of building upon their rubble a future that we all want to live and believe in. A future that is ours to care for now.

1 Marea Creciente Mexico, chapter member of Rising Tide North America, and the international Rising Tide grassroots network for Climate Justice: www.marea-creciente.org, www.risingtidenorthamerica.org, www.risingtideworldwide.org. The phrase in quotations is taken from the tag line of the Rising Tide North America logo and mission statement.

2 UNFCC – **www.unfccc.int**

3 Quote taken from various interviews given by Tom B.K. Goldtooth, director of the Indigenous Environmental Network – **www.ien.org**

4 Lee Kyung-Hae – **www.asianfarmers.org/?page_id=536**

5 Asamblea Nacional de Afectados Ambientales, in Spanish – **www.afectadosambientales.org**

6 PROFEPA – Procuraduria Federal de Proteccion Ambiental – **www.profepa.gob.mx**

The Body of the Image, or towards a Communist Art Practice

by Alexander Dunst

During the initial planning stage of the collective art project "El Martillo", someone remembered a quote, attributed variously to Bertolt Brecht, Vladimir Mayakovsky, or even Karl Marx: "Art is not a mirror held up to reality but a hammer with which to shape it". The quote became a frequent reference point during the later stages of the hammer's construction in the small art space Organ Kritischer Kunst (OKK) in Berlin's working class district of Wedding, a rather grim area of pre- and post-war tenements, and one of the city's poorest and most ethnically diverse. Despite its obvious pertinence for the project, a number of participants were visibly uncomfortable with the prominence the quote assumed at this stage. This discomfort seemed to centre on Mayakovsky's but also, to a lesser degree Brecht's, ideological proximity to Soviet Communism. In what follows, I will return to the quote and this feeling of unease but argue that, to the contrary, any political art today is by necessity communist art – if not quite in the way that produced such strong feelings in some participants.

Take this as my thesis – and I'll explain in more detail below what I mean by it – but let us return, first, to the hammer and its gestation out of earlier work by Artúr van Balen and Jakub Simcik. As I understand it, the project evolved from Artúr and Jakub's experience of the Climate Change Conference in Copenhagen in 2009. This seems to have been an experience of exclusion, of the reduction to spectatorship, documented in Jakub's film of their bicycle trip to Denmark. What they experience there are two closed circuits of mediatisation, of media spectacle, as it were. On the one hand, beleaguered and hermetically sealed off, the negotiations about the future of planet Earth – the realm of the political by definition, one might think, but so removed from the decisions that would safeguard our future as if the assembled politicians and bureaucrats wanted to prove, once and for all, the retreat of institutional politics from any collective responsibility and action. On the other hand, freezing and intimidated by the police, the assembled protesters and NGOs. Both vie for attention, for air time and headlines in the international media – which is also the only meeting place of these two circuits accessible to those affected by the outcome of the summit – affected yet distant, spectators not participants.

The hammer is then a critical response to this experience of impotence – or, to be precise, an ironic one. The ironies are complex. The protest hammer, a huge, shiny, imposing object filled with nothing but hot air is built from the impotence of a protest culture as spectacle, a protest culture whose energies are routinely absorbed by the circuits of the world's media corporations – Bertelsmann and Murdoch, Springer and CNN – yet the hammer continues to invest into exactly these circuits.

This is one irony, but I mention it not solely to criticise the project. Rather, I think it brings us to the constitutive ambivalence of the spectacular as such, or more simply, of the image. The image, as the psychoanalyst Jacques Lacan understands it, lures us into a mistaken conviction of completion, of fullness, of the ultimate satisfaction of our desires. It establishes a continuous succession of images that ironically fuels our desire by promising an end to it, its satisfaction. However the image also, and perhaps more decisively, brings the body into being. As Lacan proposes in his famous essay on the mirror stage, at some point the child recognises him- or herself in the mirror, that is to say, *mis*recognises herself for a two-dimensional image, and thus for the first time constructs a body, produces a bordered territory of sensations out of its real flesh.[1] This body wrongly promises a state of fullness or completion, but it is also the only body we will ever have.

A body, then, is the construction of an image, and to produce an image is to produce a body. For what else is the hammer but a body, a shaped form and representational figure. At the same time, the hammer's size already indicates its supra-individual aim, the production of the collective, or body, of protesters. This function of the hammer's function can perhaps best be accounted for with reference to Kafka's famous tale "Josephine the Singer, or the Mouse Folk".[2] As Kafka tells us, the oppressed mice people regularly gather to hear Josephine sing. Yet Josephine does not sing so well – some even question whether she can sing at all or simply whistles like all other mice do – nor will her name be remembered after her death. But even in times of great danger, and perhaps particularly under such circumstances, do the mice assemble around her fragile voice, to forget their sorrows, and to come together as one people. Kafka's story should be read precisely as an account of communist art. Josephine's art consists entirely in the production of the mice people as a collective, in allowing for the production and organisation of the commons. It is solely in this act that Josephine's singing is spectacular, is imaginary, and constructs a body – a body that cannot, by definition, survive its moment of realisation.[3]

I'd like to close by mentioning another, and perhaps the most obvious, irony of the project, which returns us to Mayakovsky's quote: "Art is not a mirror held up to reality but a hammer with which to shape it". What lurks behind the uncomfortable associations with Soviet Communism is, of course, not the laughable implication that either Brecht or Majakoswki bore any responsibility for the horrendous crimes of Stalinism, but that it reminds us of the Leninist instrumentalisation of violence, in which the destruction of the old was to become the production of the new.

The protest hammer, as I mentioned earlier, is a hammer made of air and plastic foil. But this does not mean that the hammer is not an instrument of violence, nor should art refrain from engaging in violence. It's probably the opposite: art has to be violent. But this is a violence that is symbolic rather than ontological: a violence that does not express itself in the harming of the body and the destruction of objects but in the dissolution of established knowledge and the perception of the hitherto invisible. In part at least, art in general – and the hammer in particular – perpetrates an ironic violence. For irony, to return to Lacan once more, undermines authority by questioning its omnipotence: its existence independently of the continuous supply of our affect and our labour that sustains it.
To put it simply, the potential of a piece of political art, like the protest hammer, lies in the simultaneous production of the collective and the questioning of the omnipotence of media spectacle. It seems to me that it is the indivisibility of these two aspects of the hammer, its paradoxical nature as an ironic body, on which its appeal for the protesters at Cancún and its obvious threat to the police was built. Thus whilst it brings the shared body of protesters into being, in its practical deployment the hammer also subverts another body, that of state apparatuses in their imaginary sense of totality.

In a move that belies any division between ecology and politics, industrial and developing countries alike have been pushing to turn our remaining natural resources into commodities. Clean air and green forests will be traded and sold against pollution and destruction. It is in this precise sense that the major questions facing us today – climate change, biodiversity, equality – depend on political decisions that pit a communism of the commons, of the last natural resources shared without ownership, against the further expansion of capitalism. Such an "idea of communism", as Alain Badiou has recently called it, asserts its continuing validity against the very real failures of Stalinism and rejects its wholesale ideological denunciation stemming from the Cold War.[4] In this defense and production of the commons an ironic distance from state apparatuses such as the corporate media functions as an important tactic. Here, art can either be part of that spectacular mirror we call reality, or a hammer with which to shape it anew.

1 Jacques Lacan, "The Mirror Stage as Formative of the *I* Function as Revealed in Psychoanalytic Experience", in *Ecrits: The First Complete Edition in English*. Translated by Bruce Fink (New York: Norton, 2002), 75–81.

2 Franz Kafka, "Josefine, die Sängerin oder Das Volk der Mäuse", in Franz Kafka. *Sämtliche Werke* (Frankfurt: Suhrkamp, 2008), 897–912.

3 Fredric Jameson, "Kafka's Dialectic", in Fredric Jameson, *Modernist Papers* (London and New York: Verso, 2007), 96–112.

4 See Alain Badiou's *The Communist Hypothesis* as well as the essay collection *The Idea of Communism* for an extended discussion. These attempts to re-introduce the term into political debate and counteract its demonisation build on the conviction that it cannot be reduced to its hijacking by certain dictatorships and conservative Western ideologues and uniquely conveys practices and concepts central to any rejuvenation of a radical left politics: from the abolition of classes and the profit motive, to shared production and ownership, as well as the free expression of creativity. Alain Badiou, *The Communist Hypothesis* (London and New York: Verso, 2010); and Slavoj Žižek and Costas Douzinas (eds.), *The Idea of Communism* (London and New: Verso, 2010).

On the Phenomenology of Giant Puppets

Excerpt

by David Graeber

David Graeber is an anthropologist who lectures at Goldsmith College in London, UK. His essay "On the Phenomenology of Giant Puppets" makes an analysis of the culture and relationship between protesters and the police in the United States.

Graeber examines the symbolism of these puppets and analyses the police's aversion to them. Unlike the "black bloc", easily infiltrated by undercover police informers and stigmatised as being exclusively violent, the puppets transform the protest into a festive celebration of an alternative world that is harder for the police to control. He observes, "police strategies aim to destroy or capture the puppets before they can even appear on the streets".

What follows, is an excerpt from his book "Possibilities", authorised by David Graeber.

WHAT THEN OF PUPPETS?

Again, they seem the perfect complement. Giant papier mâché puppets are created by taking the most ephemeral of material – ideas, paper, wire mesh – and transforming it into something very like a monument, even if they are, at the same time, somewhat ridiculous. A giant puppet is the mockery of the idea of a monument, and of everything monuments represent: the inapproachability, monochrome solemnity, above all the implication of permanence, the state's (itself ultimately somewhat ridiculous) attempt to turn its principle and history into eternal verities. If one is meant to shatter the existing Spectacle, the other is, it seems to me, to suggest the permanent capacity to create new ones.

In fact, from the perspective of the activists, it is again process – in this case, the process of production – that is really the point. There are brainstorming sessions to come up with themes and visions, organizing meetings, but above all, the wires and frames lie on the floors of garages or yards or warehouses or similar quasi-industrial spaces for days, surrounded by buckets of paint and construction materials, almost never alone, with small teams in attendance, molding, painting, smoking, eating, playing music, arguing, wandering in and out. Everything is designed to be communal, egalitarian, expressive. The objects themselves are not expected to last. They are for the most part made of fairly delicate materials; few would withstand a heavy rainstorm; some are even self-consciously destroyed or set ablaze in the course of actions. Even otherwise, in the absence of permanent storage facilities, they usually quickly start to fall apart.

As for the images: these are clearly meant to encompass, and hence constitute, a kind of universe. Normally Puppetistas, as they sometimes call themselves, aim for a rough balance between positive and negative images. On the one hand, one might have the Giant Pig that represents the World Bank, on the other, a Giant Liberation Puppet whose arms can block an entire highway. Many of the most famous images identify marchers and the things they wear or carry: for instance, a giant bird puppet at A16 (the 2000 IMF/World Bank actions) was accompanied by hundreds of little birds on top of signs distributed to all and sundry. Similarly, Haymarket martyrs, Zapatistas, the Statue of Liberty, or a Liberation Monkeywrench might carry slogans identical to those carried on the signs, stickers, or T-shirts of those actually taking part in the action:

The most striking images though are often negative ones: the corporate control puppet at the 2000 democratic convention, operating both Bush and Gore like marionettes, a giant riot policeman who shoots out pepper spray, and endless effigies to be encompassed and ridiculed.

The mocking and destruction of effigies is of course one of the oldest and most familiar gestures of political protest. Often such effigies are an explicit assault on monumentality. The fall of regimes are marked by the pulling down of statues; it was the (apparently staged) felling of the statue of Saddam Hussein in Baghdad that, in the minds of almost everyone, determined the moment of the actual end of his regime. Similarly, during George Bush's visit to England in 2004, protestors built innumerable mock statues of Bush, large and small, just in order to pull them down again.

Still, the positive images are often treated with little more respect than the effigies. Here is an extract from my early reflections on the subject, jotted down shortly after spending time in the Puppet Warehouse in Philadelphia before the Republican Convention in 2000, somewhat re-edited.

FIELD NOTES EXTRACTS, JULY 31ST, 2000

The question I keep asking myself is: why are these things even called "puppets"?

Normally one thinks of "puppets" as figures that move in response to the motions of some puppeteer.

Most of these have few if any moving parts. These are more light moving statues, sometimes worn, sometimes carried. So in what sense are they "puppets"?

Puppets are extremely visual, large, but also delicate and ephemeral. Usually they fall apart after a single action. This combination of huge size and lightness seems to me makes them a bridge between words and reality; they are the point of transition; they represent the ability to start to make ideas real and take on solid form, to make our view of the world into something of equal physical bulk and greater spectacular power even to the engines of state violence that stand against it. The idea that they are extensions of our minds, words, make help explain the use of the term "puppets". They may not move around as an extension of some individual's will. But if they did, this would somewhat contradict the emphasis on collective creativity. Insofar as they are characters in a drama, it is a drama with a collective author; insofar as they are manipulated, it is in a sense by everyone, in processions, often passed around from one activist to the next. Above all they are meant to be emanations of a collective imagination. As such, for them either to become fully solid, or fully manipulable by a single individual, would contradict the point.

Puppets can be worn like costumes, and in large actions, they are in fact continuous with costumes.

Every major mobilization had its totem, or totems: the famous sea-turtles at Seattle, the birds and sharks at A16, the Dancing Skeletons at R2K (the Republican Convention in Philly), the caribou at Bush's inauguration, or for that matter, the fragments of Picasso's Guernica designed for the protests against the upcoming Iraq invasion in 2003, designed so that they could each wander off and then all periodically combine together.

In fact, there's usually no clear line between puppets, costumes, banners and symbols, and simple props. Everything is designed to overlap and reinforce each other. Puppets tend to be surrounded by a much larger "carnival bloc", replete with clowns, stilt-walkers, jugglers, fire-breathers, unicyclists, Radical Cheerleaders, costumed kick-lines or often, entire marching bands – such as the Infernal Noise Brigade of the Bay Area or Hungry March Band in New York – that usually specialize in klezmer or circus music, in addition to the ubiquitous drums and whistles. The circus metaphor seems to sit particularly well with anarchists, presumably because circuses are collections of extreme individuals (one can't get much more individualistic than a collection of circus freaks) nonetheless engaged in a purely cooperative enterprise that also involves transgressing ordinary boundaries. Tony Blair's famous comment in 2004 that he was not about to be swayed by "some traveling anarchist circus" was not taken, by many, as an insult. There are in fact quite a number of explicitly anarchist circus troupes, their numbers only matched, perhaps, by that of various phoney preachers. The connection is significant; for now, the critical thing is that every action will normally have its circus fringe, a collection of flying squads that circulate through the large street blockades to lift spirits, perform street theater, and also, critically, to try to defuse moments of tension or potential conflict. This latter is crucial. Since direct-actions, unlike permitted marches, scrupulously avoid marshals or formal peace-keepers (who police will always try to co-opt), the puppet/circus squads often end up serving some of the same functions. Here is a first-hand account by members of one such affinity group from Chapel Hill ("Paper Hand Puppet Intervention") about how this might work itself out in practice.

"Burger and Zimmerman brought puppets to the explosive protests of the World Trade Organization in Seattle two years ago, where they joined a group that was blockading the building in which talks were being held. "People had linked arms" Zimmerman says. "The police had beaten and pepper-sprayed them already, and they threatened that they were coming back in five minutes to attack them again." But the protestors held their line, linking arms and crying, blinded by the pepper spray. Burger, Zimmerman and their friends came along – on stilts, with clowns, a 40-foot puppet, and a belly dancer. They went up and down the line, leading the protesters in song. When the security van returned, they'd back the giant puppet up into its way. Somehow, this motley circus diffused the situation. "They couldn't bring themselves to attack this bunch of people who were now singing songs" Zimmerman says. Injecting humour and celebration into a grim situation, he says, is the essence of a puppet intervention.

For all the circus trappings, those most involved in making and deploying giant puppets will often insist that they are deeply serious. "Puppets are not cute, like muppets" insists Peter Schumann, the director of Bread and Puppet Theater – the group historically most responsible for popularizing the use of papier-mâché figures in political protest in the '60s. "Puppets are effigies and gods and meaningful creatures". Sometimes, they are literally so: as with the Maya gods that came to greet delegates at the WTO meetings in Cancún in September 2003. Always, they have a certain numinous quality. Still, if giant puppets, generically, are gods, most are obviously, foolish, silly, ridiculous gods. It is as if the process of producing and displaying puppets becomes a way to both seize the power to make gods, and to make fun of it at the same time. Here one seems to be striking against a profoundly anarchist sensibility. Within anarchism, one encounters a similar impulse at every point where one approaches the mythic or deeply meaningful. It appears to be operative in the doctrines of Zerzanites and similar Primitivists, who go about self-consciously creating myths (their own version of the Garden of Eden, the Fall, the coming Apocalypse), that seem to imply they want to see millions perish in a worldwide industrial collapse, or that they seek to abolish agriculture or even language – then bridle at the suggestion that they really do. It's clearly present in the writings of theorists like Peter Lamborn Wilson, whose meditations on the role of the sacred in revolutionary action are written under the persona of an insane Ismaili pederastic poet named Hakim Bey. It's even more clearly present among Pagan anarchist groups like Reclaiming, who since the anti-nuclear movement of the '80s,[1] have specialized in conducting what often seem like extravagant satires of pagan rituals that they nonetheless insist are real rituals which are really effective – even, that represent what they see as the deepest possible spiritual truths about the world.[2]

Puppets simply push this logic to a kind of extreme. The sacred here is, ultimately, the sheer power of creativity, of the imagination – or, perhaps more exactly, the power to bring the imagination into reality. This is, after all, the ultimate ideal of all revolutionary practice, to, as the '68 slogan put it, "give power to the imagination." But it is also as if the democratization of the sacred can only be accomplished through a kind of burlesque. Hence the constant self-mockery, which, however, is never meant to genuinely undercut the gravity and importance of what's being asserted, but rather, to imply the ultimate recognition that just because gods are human creations they are still gods, and that taking this fact too seriously might prove dangerous.

1 Barbara Epstein, *Political Protest and Cultural Revolution: Non-violent Direct Action in the 1970s and 1980s.* Berkeley: University of California Press, 1991.

2 The Pagan Bloc has been a regular fixture in large-scale actions since Seattle, and, unlike the Quakers and other Christian proponents of civil disobedience, was willing, ultimately, to recognize Black Bloc practice as a form of non-violence and even to form a tacit alliance with them.

Against Representation

Interview with John Jordan

by Artúr van Balen, Jakub Simcik and Pablo Hermann

UK-based John Jordan has been experimenting with the borderline between art and activism since the late 1980's. He was the co-director of the art collective "Platform" (1987 – 1995) and co-founder of the well known group "Reclaim the Streets" (1995 – 2000), who organised the "Carnival Against Capitalism" in 1999: a seminal event that helped shape global protest culture for a whole generation. In the last couple of years he has been working under the group moniker "The Laboratory of Insurrectionary Imagination". The Laboratory has made itself a name through such spectacular actions as the formation of "C.I.R.C.A" (Clandestine Insurgent Rebel Clown Army), revealed in time for the 2005 G8 in Scotland. In 2009 they organised the "Bike Bloc" intervention at the Copenhagen climate conference in 2009, in which some members from the Eclectic Electric Collective participated.

The "Laboratory of Insurrectionary Imagination" has inspired us in many ways: in thinking about the relationship of art and activism, while pragmatically creating highly engaging, and deeply democratic group processes. in which some members from the Eclectic Electric Collective participated.

In spring 2011 we met up with John Jordan in the "Haus der Kulturen der Welt" in Berlin to discuss his view on the relationship between art and activism.

It seems that the work of Joseph Beuys' work has had an enormous impact on you. What was the appeal?

I suppose Joseph Beuys made me realise the connection between art and politics. What I found interesting about his work was that it was an aesthetic doorway into politics. If you look at the work that I do now with the collectives I work with, we're actually trying to create a doorway into radical politics, a doorway that doesn't necessarily *look* like radical politics. It looks like art, it looks like bicycles, it looks like clowns.

Interestingly, I came upon Beuys through shamanism. What fascinated me were the practices of travel: the idea of the shaman as a character that could travel between different worlds, the shaman as an in-between figure. So, in a sense it was Beuys, shamanism, and social sculpture that drew me into an understanding that the material of artistic practice should be society. I think that it's interesting how he used the art world and the art market to create capital that he would then divert into other places, like the Green Party or the student movements. But I'm also quite critical of his use of the ego and of the image of the "individual genius artist" – which is clearly problematic when it comes to radical politics.

There seems to be different approaches to reforming parliamentarian democracy. Roughly said, one of them could be reforming it from the "inside", i.e. by accepting the rules of the game and getting politically involved in political parties. Another example could be from the "outside", perhaps through direct action and through the foundation of temporary autonomous zones. Also, there is the question of what role could art play in radical politics? What is your stand on these questions?

Those are the big magic questions *(laughs)* to which there are many answers. What I've learned through my engagement with the anti-globalisation movement and the Zapatistas is this idea of plurality. This escape from a single ideological position and from a single set of tools – to one that is much more complex, much more based on local knowledge, based on local situations and local context.

What I think is interesting are the edges, which is a concept that I've learned from ecology. The edges of eco-systems are situated at places such as seashores, and these are places where you will find the biggest number of inter-relationships between different forms of species. When you have such diversity, you have more creativity and more evolution. These kinds of eco-systems have enormous amounts of inter-pollution and creativity. I think that it's really interesting as artists and activists to ask ourselves "How do we create those edges?" Not as dialogue, because I don't give a fuck about having a "dialogue" with those in power. It's not about demanding them to change but about creating situations where they are affected, as well as people outside of the system. Change comes from outside of the system, from the edges, and our role as artists and activists is to work there. If you look at anything that we take for granted – like women wearing trousers – once upon a time it used to be totally illegal and weird! Women were killed for wearing trousers! But it was women on the edges of the system in subcultures a hundred years ago that started wearing them and now it's considered normal!

During our hammer making workshop, one of the participants noted "Ambiguity is good for arts but bad for protests". We think that this is the main tension between artists and protesters because strong artistic works are always ambiguous, whereas social groups always strive for a clear message. How do you deal with this issue?

Most of the work we do is to create spaces where artists and activists can meet. A space that combines the courage, social critique, and clarity of the activists, and on the other hand the ambiguity, imagination, and poetics of the artists. The search for new ways of doing political or artistic action is really important for the work that we do with the Laboratory of Insurrectionary Imagination. But the question of ambiguity is really interesting. Artists are really terrified of being instrumentalised. Artists claim their autonomy, their freedom as the basis of their artistic practice. But the fact that most artists are completely instrumental in creating an art market by creating cultural capital and thus enabling capitalism to exist and to seem innovative – that is by most artists not seen as being instrumental. On the other hand, if you lose the ambiguity, then you're not using the power that artists can bring to the process of activism – and you end up with propaganda. Propaganda has no ambiguity. Instead I am interested in political action that has both clarity and ambiguity. I know that somehow sounds meaningless, but I think that the key is that it shouldn't feel like a political action. I think that the clown army is an interesting example, since it was so paradoxical: were these people clowns or were they activists? Was this fun or was it direct action? Did it have a function or was it simply decoration, was it simply a spectacle? It's all about the edge between ambiguity and propaganda.

The Zapatistas talk a lot about the politics of paradox, and that's how I like to see it too. "How do you create paradoxical situations?" is a question I often ask myself. It would be very sad to lose ambiguity in radical politics but I think that it would be equally sad to have the level of ambiguity of most contemporary art, which can be so fucking ambiguous that it becomes isolated in its own cultural space. That's why I think that artists and activists coming together can find that space, because you're bound to go through exciting negotiations, at the end of which you hopefully have something that works. I mean – look at advertising! Advertising is filled with ambiguity – that's why it works! In the end it makes us desire, it gives us a space to fill with our desires to be channelled, into capital.

The key to ambiguity is that it creates levels of participation. And I think that activists in their desire for clarity actually forget that the clearer you are, the less space there is for the spectator, or the reader, or the participant – to actually *participate*. Because it's finished. The meaning is finished, it's there and it's all sealed off. But when you create ambiguity, you can start to create a space of participation, and that's the importance of ambiguity.

From our own experience we've noticed how difficult it is to engage political activists in poetic action. The typical scope of action seems only to effect the organisation of marches and the making of banners with more or less pertinent slogans.

Activists still think that we're in the 1950's. There's not enough deconstruction and semiotics of the way that advertising works. In itself it could be interesting to do workshops with activists on marketing and show its efficiency to them. For me the ideas of Stephen Duncombe holds an appeal: of creating dreams of what could be. Creating spectacles that feel and look like the world that you're trying to create. That in itself will always be ambiguous because you wouldn't want that new world that you're trying to create to be completely fixed and sealed. For me it's all about creating situations in which people behave like they're in the world that they want to be in, but where they also feel how that world would feel like. It's a micro-strategy on how one could use certain forms of art and activism together. As artists that's what we have to do, we have to construct desire, the desire for people to engage in radical politics in their everyday life, in forms of making and living.

There was a lot of hope and a lot of mobilisation efforts in front of the COP 15 climate conference in Copenhagen in 2009. Did the failures of COP 15 make you reconsider your strategy?

I think that the COP 15 affected a lot of people's thinking around strategy and effectiveness. I think that the key is to always think *resistance-alternative*.

The danger for utopian communities to become nothing but laboratories of capitalism is especially there with green capitalism – if they're not also resisting. Copenhagen really reminded me that we need to bring those two together. We did a Bike Bloc project there, where we picked up 500 dead bikes from the streets of Copenhagen and then organised open workshops in galleries and social centres about how to turn a bike into a tool of civil disobedience. COP 15 also made me re-think symbolic action. It made me want to return to actions that actually manage to stop something – instead of actions that symbolically stop something. To really be blocking the machine, but to be blocking it with something that presents the alternative – that's a challenge! To block the machine with a really beautiful thing.

We wanted to ask you about the funding of activist projects. Obviously, there is a thin line there as you might find yourself being sponsored by the very corporations or institutions that you are opposing. There is

the constant risk of getting co-opted. How do you deal with that? Did you ever mask your past projects, such as your involvement with Reclaim the Streets in the 90's, in order to get funding?

It depends on the context. The Re-Think exhibition that we were supposed to do in 2009 poses an interesting case: We were commissioned to do a project on the Copenhagen climate summit by the contemporary art museum in Copenhagen as part of an exhibition around climate and politics. I sent a proposal, which very clearly said, "We will transform bicycles into tools of civil disobedience." I think that the words "civil disobedience" were probably there, six times in the proposal. They'd seen our website, they knew the work we do. Then at one point we were telephoning and they told us that we can't weld in the gallery because of health and safety issues. Which was fine, because we could just put a welding container outside of the art space. Then the curator rang me up and told me that she'd just been talking to the police. In Denmark there's a rule about what a bicycle can be in terms of size, measurements etc. I told her that it doesn't really matter what the rules about bicycles are, because we were going to be doing civil disobedience anyway, and probably be breaking the laws. And she was completely flabbergasted: "You're going to be breaking the law?!" That was an incredible moment where I realised the tyranny of representation in the art world is to such an extent where you'll even give someone a proposal which repeatedly talks about "civil disobedience" and you show them the history of your work but still they're going to think that you're simply going to represent politics, that you're going to make images of politics, but that you're not going to be doing politics. So they tried to change it, and in the end we split with them.

But, for me the key question is cultural capital. I think that as a political artist one has to be really careful and keep in mind that it's both a funding and a toxin. It's a poison and it can go against the political aims of the project that you're doing. But it's at the same time a way of getting agency. I think one has to be very careful, and for me the key question is to ask: "What is our ethical-political position?" – and to never give that up! Never make a difference! A month ago I met with an interesting artist who had done a project in Mannheim. She had begun with the Tute Bianchi in Italy, and she had also been in the anti-globalisation movement. She used to say "In those days I had my politics and I had my art. I had my art practice and it wasn't political, and I had my politics and it was separate."

But as she stopped her political engagement, her arts practice became more socially engaged. She was showing us a big gentrification project that she had done, which had been commissioned by Theater der Welt and the development agency that was doing the gentrification. This project of hers was mildly critical of gentrification, working with lots of people affected by gentrification, like biker gangs, punk bands, and people who lived by the port. "You have cultural capital for your art project against gentrification funded by the art world, surely your cultural capital is going to help the process of gentrification, rather than hinder it?" I asked her. "Well, yeah, but I'm interested in dialogue. I want to bring everyone together for dialogue" she responded.

Classic! Classic thing in the art world – the fear of conflict! The idea that dialogue is the resolution to social change, not conflict. I told her, that gentrification is an incredibly violent activity. It pushes people out of their homes, it forces people to move somewhere else. It has a violent effect on people's lives. "Are you against or for gentrification, and did the project help it?", I pressured her. "Personally," she said, "of course I'm against gentrification, but in my art it's a different thing." That's when it suddenly became clear for me what the problem is in the art world. The people have certain personal ethics but their art is somehow separate from that. In my opinion, capitalism is a separation of all our activities into little bits. If one is to begin thinking about post-capitalist culture, then it's a process of integrating, integrating aesthetics into ethics. The question is: How do you do that without making compromises? The answer is, that often you have to sabotage your own cultural capital. To sabotage your own role as an artist, even though, you know that you won't get invited back. For example, I know that I will never ever be invited back to the Tate Gallery – ever – because of what we did there. Which is fine by me! But there was a moment of realisation during that project for me, and it was never a question of what I would choose, because for me the politics are always more important than the ego, more important than the cultural capital. You can always play that game to get funding, but as soon as you think that that funding is promoting capital or promoting part of the problem that you're against – to be able to pull out.

The key is awareness of cultural capital. Is your cultural capital going to help capital? And at what point is your cultural capital going to go against capital? It's not easy, but I don't believe that you shouldn't be taking public money, because it's public money! I don't think that you should take corporate money, under any circumstances. I can't imagine a situation where I would feel ethically able to take it.

Berlin, 25.11.2010

Press Release

Berlin collective sends gigantic Protest-Hammer to Cancún Climate Conference.

We see art not as a mirror to hold up to reality but as a hammer with which to shape it.
– Bertolt Brecht

„El Martillo", is a twelve meters tall, inflatable silver sculpture, which was made in Berlin by the artist group "Eclectic Electric Collective" and which has been sent to Mexico for the Cancún Climate Conference protests. El martillo expresses the need to create bonds of solidarity accross the globe and to smash climate change.
It will be inflated on the 30.11.2010 at the convergence of social movements for climate justice at the Angel de la Indepencia. It will then travel with the climate procession from Mexico City to Cancún to join the action in Cancún at 6.11.2010 Día de Acción contra el Capitalismo Verde y los Megaproyectos (Day against green capitalism and mega projects).

Why a hammer? Reasons vary with each member of the group:

Sarah Drain, Eclectic Electric Collective:
With the hammer we wanted to create an icon for all the different social movements that gather in Cancún for the climate conference protests. It is also an expression of solidarity, because without the support we received in Germany and Mexico this project would not have been possible.

Artúr van Balen, Eclectic Electric Collective:
El Martillo is like the Trojan horse. The hammer was smuggled into Mexico in order to attract attention to the protests during the climate conference in Cancún. After the failure of COP 15, there is almost no media interest in what is happening in Cancún, although the UN negotiations are of vital importance for future generations on this planet.

After „El Martillo" was put into action on the 15.10 2010 at the „Global Day of Action for Climate Justice" in Leipzig, the gigantic hammer was folded into a small inconspicious travellers´ suitcase and transported from Berlin to Mexico City. Here it has been picked up by members of the group „Marea Creciente Mexico" („Rising tide Mexico").

In the link are press quality photos of „El Martillo" in action in Leipzig and Berlin and Mexico City from the 19.11. For more information, contact us in Mexico or in Germany under the following adresses:

Environmental organisation:
Marea Creciente Mexico
-contacto regional centro-
www.marea-creciente.org
mareacreciente@gmail.com

Cristian Guerrero (spanish and english speaking)

Berlin artist group:
Eclectic Electric Collective
www.eclectic-electric-collective.blogspot.com

Artúr van Balen (dutch, english, german speaking)

> From: “Andreas Knobloch”, Freier Journalist in Cancún
> Subject: El Martillo
> Date: 3 Dec 2010 17:53:04 -0500
> To: “Artúr van Balen” <arturelectrico@gmail.com>

| Kann Kunst helfen neue Protestformen zu finden oder ist sie bereits eine Form von Protest?

A:Kommerzielle Galerie-Kunst speißt Protest nicht.
Wie die Londoner Künstler-Aktivisten Gruppe „Laboratory of Insurectionary Imagination“ glauben wir aber, dass man mithilfe kreativer Selbstorganisation Protestformen und Happenings entwickeln kann, die unvorhersehbar und spektakulär sind, und die auf diesem Weg soziale Bewegungen unterstützen können.
Ein Nebeneffekt dieser partizipativen „Happenings“, wie zum Beispiel „The Bike Bloc“ bei der Reclaim Power-Demonstration während des Kopenhagener Klimagipfels oder den Castor Protesten ist, dass sie einen gemeinsamen Erfahrungshorizont schaffen. Das wirkt wieder verbrüdernd für zukünftige Aktionen.
J:Eine Lehre die wir aus unseren Erfahrungen in Schottland und in Kopenhagen gezogen haben, ist, dass Aktivismus mit der Produktion von Bildern zu tun hat. Bei jeder direkten Aktion waren ungefähr zwanzig bis dreißig Prozent der Menschen vor Ort, um zu fotografieren oder um zu filmen. Die meisten von ihnen sahen sich auch als Aktivisten. Es schien uns, als ob die Bilder von den Protesten für viele wichtiger waren als das, was wirklich vor Ort passierte. Wenn alles sowieso für die Kameras inszeniert ist, könnte man doch etwas Bewusstsein für Form und Bild entwickeln, sodass man auf der medienpolitischen Ebene ein bisschen mehr Eindruck macht.

| Wie passen Kunst und Klimapolitik zusammen?

Kunst kann die Klimapolitik auf eine ästhetische Weise interessant machen, und die Menschen auf einer emotional argumentierenden Ebene zum Handeln anleiten. Sie verleiht Protesten eine gewisse Leichtigkeit. Der Kampf für eine sozial gerechte Welt sollte den Beteiligten auch Spaß machen.
Wir denken hier an Emma Goldmans berühmten Ausspruch: “If I can’t dance, I don’t want to be part of your revolution.”

| Muss Kunst eingreifen?

Nein, auch hier besteht die Gefahr, in Dogmen abzugleiten. Aber Kunst hat ökonomisch-politisch die Möglichkeit, zu experimentieren und alternative Situationen zu schaffen. Diese Möglichkeit sollte nicht vernachlässigt werden.

| Muss Kunst einen politischen Anspruch haben?

Nein. Kunst muss nichts, sonst wird sie zur Propaganda.
Wir sind für Biodiversität – auch in der Kunst. Zugleich versuchen wir, mit unseren Gruppen-Projekten den Mythos des individuellen Künstlers zu untergraben und unser künstlerisches Kollektiv an Klima-Aktivisten-Gruppen wie zum Beispiel Gegenstrom Berlin, anzubinden. Das ergibt dann einen gegenseitigen Austausch: wir finden, dass sie oft zu textuell und unspektakulär denken, im Gegenzug lernen wir von ihrer strategisch-politischen Planung und Bündnisarbeit.

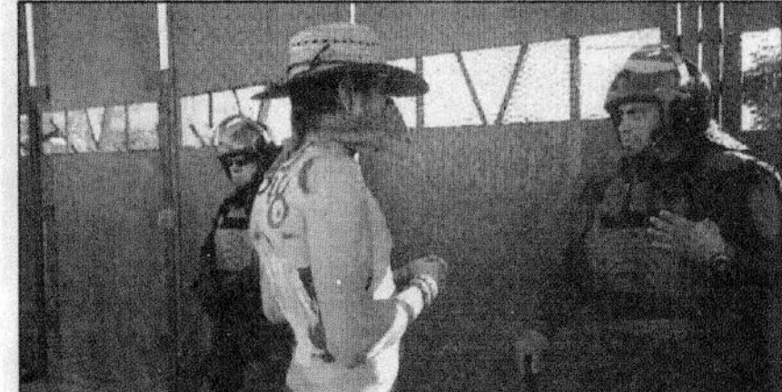

N EL CIELO, un helicóptero de la Policía Federal vigilaba y grababa sus movimientos. Asimismo, - un grupo na valla en el bulevar Luis Donaldo Colosio.

su apoyo, si no que fue todo lo contrario porque "el apoyo de ustedes me da fuerza para exigir un acuerdo justo a favor del

que ver con obligar a los pueblos contaminadores, disminuir sus emisiones de gases efecto invernadero.

mundistas, la mayoría jóvenes, decidieron ir a gritar consignas contra los agentes y el gobierno federal.

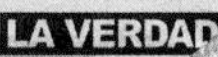

Enloquecen MARCHAS A benitojuarenses

Las diversas organizaciones ambientalistas de todo el mundo causaron tremendo caos vial al realizar multitudinarias protestas.

ROSANA DÍAZ/
GABRIEL SILVA

NOTICIAS DE CANCÚN

Tremendo caos vial ocasionaron las marchas y protestas realizadas por miles de militantes de los grupos ambientalistas altermundistas que reco-

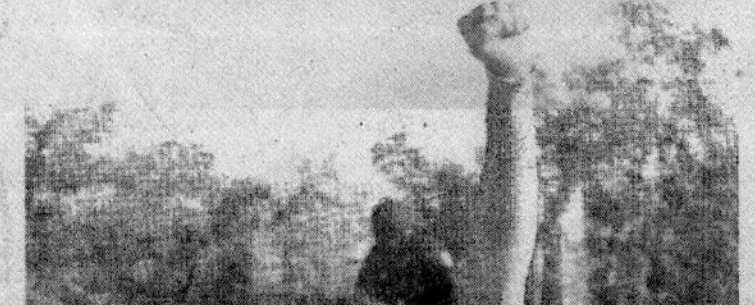

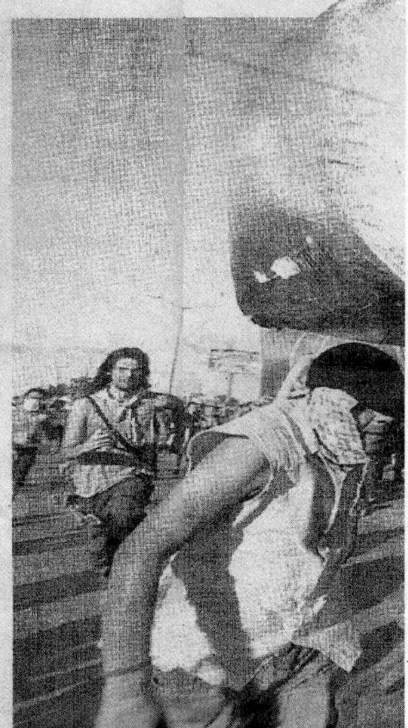

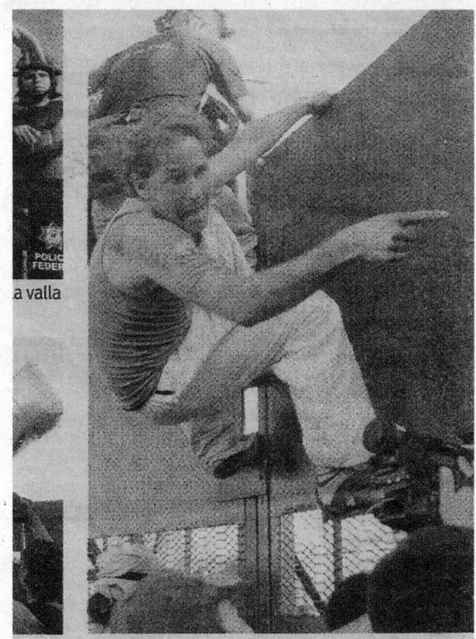

la valla metálica sin éxito.

Gran manifestación campesina

El delegado de Bolivia se unió y apoyó al grupo

SANDRA ROMERO
sromero@elperiodico.com.mx

Miles de campesinos de organizaciones tanto nacionales como internacionales, agrupados en Vía Campesina, marcharon ayer por el bulevar Luis Donaldo Colosio para exigir un acuerdo a favor de la Tierra en las negociaciones de la COP-16. En el camino, los marchistas recibieron a los delegados de Bolivia y Paraguay, Pablo Solom y Miguel Lovera, quienes expresaron que dicho movimiento fortalece la lucha que sostienen en las negociaciones oficiales.

La marcha, que concluyó en una asamblea de los pueblos en plena avenida Colosio, inició a las 9 de la mañana y partió del polifuncional "Jacinto Canek". El contingente, de aproximadamente cuatro mil personas, exclamaba consignas a favor de la Tierra como "Solución a la contaminación" y "La Tierra no se vende, la Tierra se defiende".

"007, Felipe es un ojete...009 Felipe es un culero" coreaban en referencia al presidente de la República. La intención del movimiento, explicó en su momento Alberto Gómez Flores, coordinador de Vía Campesina, fue "exigir a los gobiernos que ya se pongan a hablar del clima, porque lo que están haciendo es hablar de negocios. El clima no es un negocio".

Las negociaciones en los foros oficiales, exigió "tienen que ser conocidos por el pueblo, abiertos, porque ya es justo que se pongan hablar de cómo solucionar el problema del

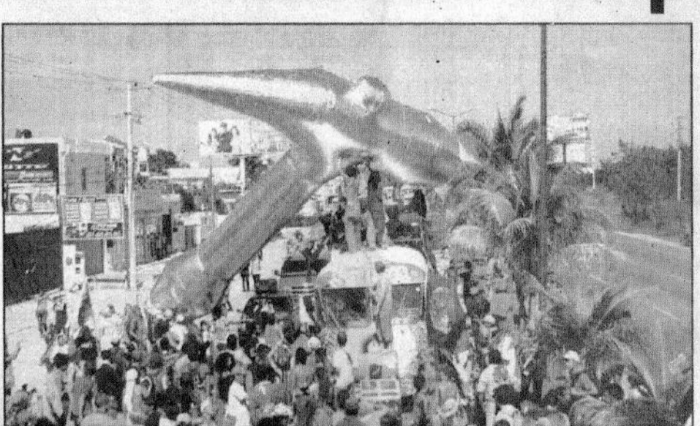

CERCA DE LAS ONCE HORAS, ya agrupados, comenzaron a caminar por todo el bulevar Luis Donaldo Colosio, algunos cantaban, otros exclamaban consignas y la delegación de Bolivia, cerca de 90 personas, entonaban canciones de su tierra.

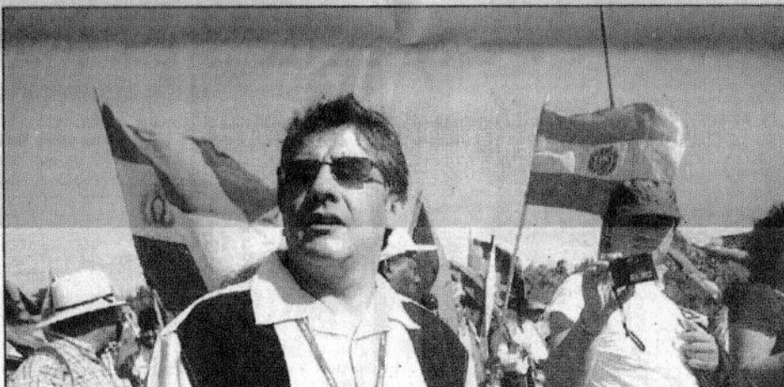

En el foro oficial, señaló, "no se debe firmar nada a escondidas, que no se esconda la realidad. No queremos recetas mediáticas", indicó.

Por su lado Miguel Lovera, delegado de Paraguay en el foro oficial, consideró que si bien las negociaciones son complicadas, "no se puede decir algo antes que esto termine. Estamos haciendo de todo con el apoyo de los pueblos en distintas partes del mundo y aquí en Cancún, para que haya un resultado satisfactorio que permita reducir las emisiones de gas de efecto invernadero de los países desarrollados y así poder estabilizar el incremento de la temperatura".

Si bien dijo que hasta el momento no hay un buen panorama, mencionó que "una negociación es como un partido de futbol, nadie puede adelantar los resultados hasta el final y hay que saber hacerlo hasta el último momento".

En las negociaciones, dijo, la mayoría de los países en desarrollo no quieren ver morir el Protocolo de Kioto, por lo cual se hará todo lo posible porque no sea así. El movimiento de los campesinos, indicó, los fortalece porque "obviamente que la voz que nosotros llevamos a las negociaciones es la voz de los pueblos que se reunieron en Cochabamba para precisamente discutir propuestas que a lo largo de todo este periodo se han vuelto temas centrales de discusión a lo largo de este proceso".

La asamblea

Los delegados marcharon por lo menos un kilómetro y medio con los altermundistas, para luego participar, en plena avenida Colosio, en la Asamblea de los Pueblos donde los representantes de distintos países participantes en la marcha, como Bolivia, Brasil, y demás, expusieron posturas ante el tema del calentamiento global y las negociaciones que se llevan al cabo en el foro oficial.

avarillas@elperiodico.com.mx

Un Cristo ensangrentado frente a la hilera de 60 elementos de la Policía Federal. Una pareja de activistas que documentan la histórica aventura, bailan tango y luego, salsa, frente a esos mismos ojos.

Un joven con taparrabos, que conmina a los azules a comprender que los reclamos que escuchan de miles de campesinos, indígenas y activistas del mundo, los incluyen a ellos y a sus hijos, como afectados por el calentamiento global.

Un grupo de mujeres de Bolivia y de Oaxaca que clama por la defensa de la Madre Tierra.

Un puñado de africanos que demandan "our lands, our rights and our sovereignty" (nuestras tierras, nuestros derechos y nuestra soberanía), junto con activistas de Tlaxcala y de Hidalgo, que se pronuncian por justicia ambiental y social, y repudian la presa construida en Tula.

Un altermundista de Dinamarca montado en una bicicleta capaz de generar su propia energía eléctrica; el "Soul Fire", autobús escolar que se alimenta de aceite comestible para viajar por el mundo, abriéndose paso entre bailes y reggae.

Una pandilla de encapuchados de negro y rojo que pinta grafiti en comercios, casas y bardas, lo mismo que en la Central de Energía Eléctrica de la Comisión Federal de Electricidad (CFE), señalada como la paraestatal que más contamina en México.

Un colosal martillo de plástico inflado, que intenta romper el cerco policiaco que frena el paso para hablar con los otros, con los representantes oficiales de países que discuten a puerta cerrada, el futuro de esos que están a fuera, pugnando por ser incluidos en aquello que les afecta directamente: El cambio climático.

Pinceladas, retratos; pequeñas piezas del rompecabezas que armaron ayer, durante más de cuatro horas, altermundistas, campesinos, indígenas y mineros, quienes viajaron desde África, Asia, Europa y Latinoamérica, para demandar

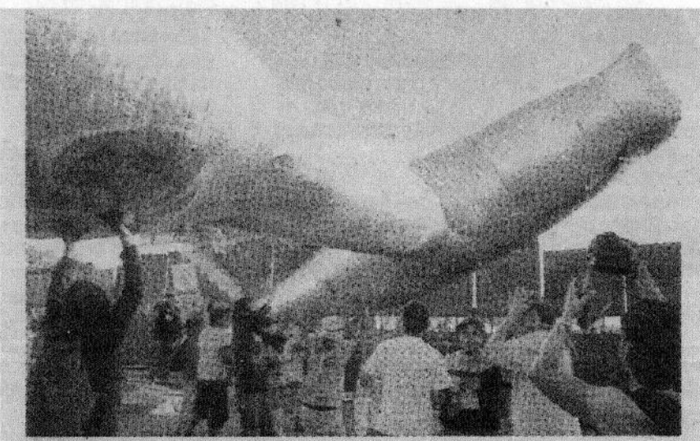

Algunos globalifóbicos radicales intentaron cruzar la valla m

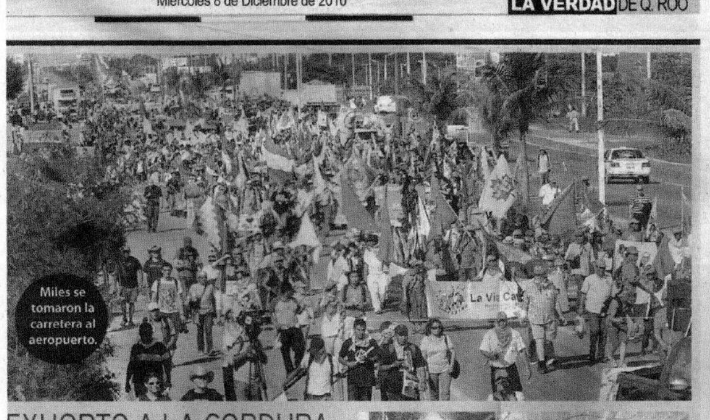

EXHORTO A LA CORDURA

No es necesario llegar a actos vandálicos para manifestar las libres ideas, por lo que quienes propicien desorden en la ciudad por la Cumbre Marco sobre Cambio Climático (COP 16) son ajenos a los grupos altermundistas,

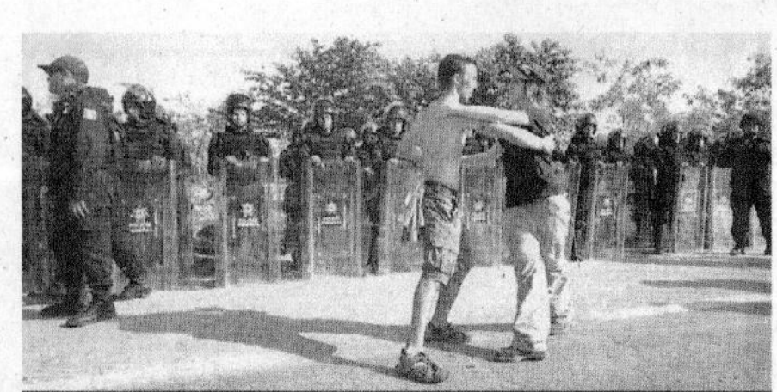

UNA PAREJA DE ACTIVISTAS que documentan la histórica aventura, bailan tango y luego, salsa, frente a esos mismos ojos.

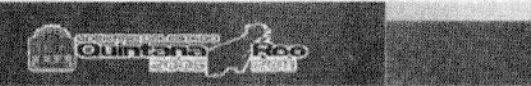

Entre los grupos, destacaban varios 'performers'.

el año 2003 en una valla de policías similar a ésta; agregó que arrojaron el mismo martillo que desde la COP 15 fue utilizado por los manifestantes alemanes, quienes se los enviaron desde Berlín, para hacer ver a los ministros que los acuerdos de la COP 16 no sirven.

Finalmente comento que el martillo no es para golpear ni agredir para las nuevas generaciones; la lucha continuará por parte de Espacio Internacional Anti-Cop.

Entre las manifestaciones de rechazo a la COP 16 y sus negociaciones en perjuicio de la vida, un manifestante de origen europeo, personificó a Jesús de Nazaret y llevó a cabo una gran actuación sobre la pasión de Cristo Jesús en

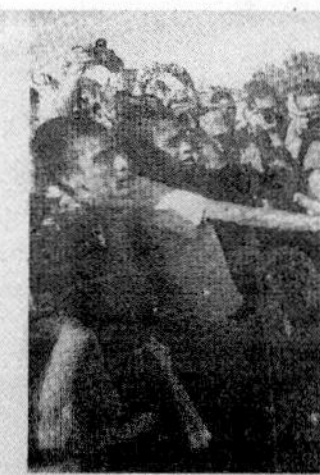

Los grupos se acercaron a l

del campamento Vía Camp marcharon desde las 8.30 l cuando salieron del Gimnasi cinto Canek y se enfilaron p Avenida Tulum hasta el Pa Municipal para abordar autob que los llevaron a la Villa Clim posteriormente avanzaron ru al aeropuerto y fueron bajad los transportes para iniciar de el poblado de Alfredo V. B

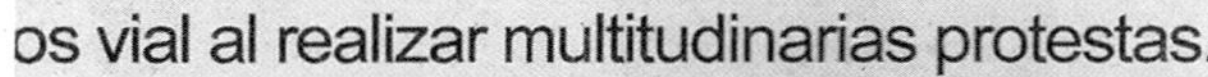

os vial al realizar multitudinarias protestas.

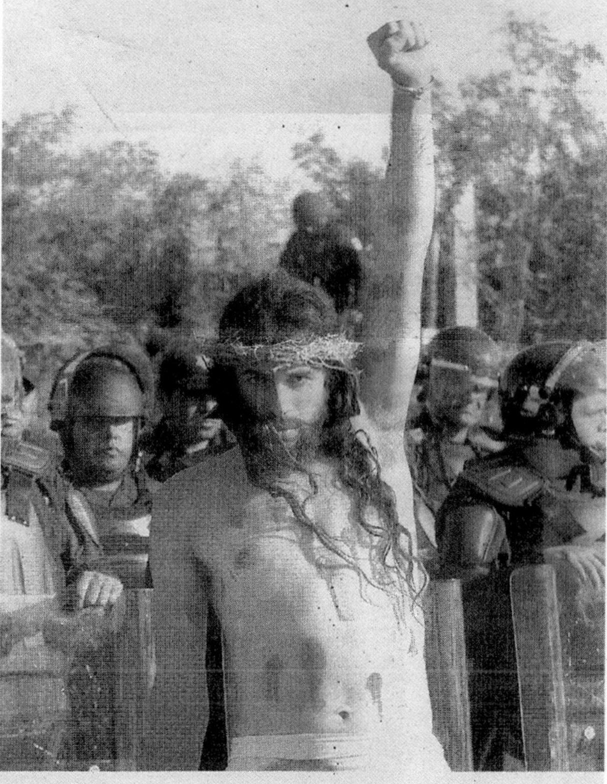

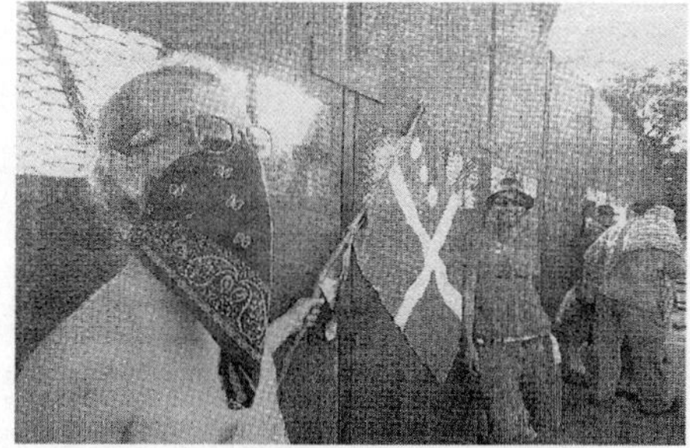

EXIGEN CAMBIAR EL SISTEMA, NO EL CLIMA

Pueblos por la Tierra

on ciones, ven tas

LAS

.com.mx

grentado frente 0 elementos de l. Una pareja de documentan la ra, bailan tango frente a esos

on taparrabos, a los azules a e los reclamos e miles de campas y activistas incluyen a ellos como afectados iento global.

le mujeres de xaca que clama de la Madre

e africanos que ar lands, our r sovereignty" , nuestros derechos oberanía), junto e Tlaxcala y de pronuncian por tal y social, y a construida en

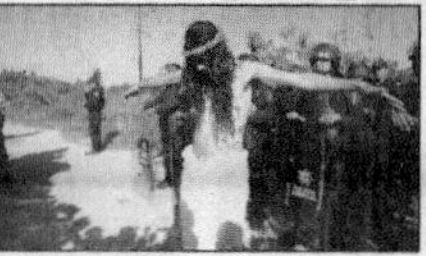

Fotos: Abner Chim

UN CRISTO ensangrentado frente a la hilera de 60 elementos de la Policía Federal. Un joven con taparrabos, que conmina a los azules a comprender que los reclamos que escuchan de miles de campesinos, indígenas y activistas del mundo, los incluyen a ellos y a sus hijos, como afectados por el calentamiento global.

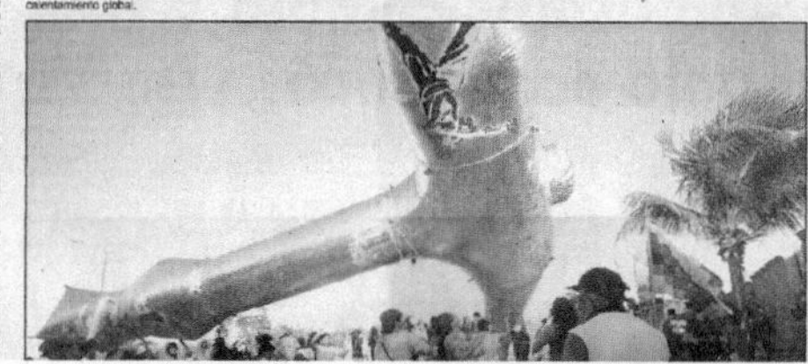

ejemplo.

"Condenamos el mecanismo REDD y REDD+ que están violando la soberanía de los pueblos y su derecho al consentimiento libre, previo e informado, así como la soberanía de Estados nacionales, y viola los derechos, usos y costumbres de los pueblos y los derechos de la naturaleza.

"Los países contaminantes están obligados a transferir de manera directa los recursos económicos y tecnológicos para pagar la restauración y mantenimiento de los bosques y selvas, a favor de los pueblos y estructuras orgánicas ancestrales indígenas, originarias, campesinas", citaban los participantes, entre consignas, amenizadas por música, bailes y color.

Carmelina Santiago Alonso, del Centro de Derechos Indígenas "Flor y Canto", en Oaxaca, lo vive en directo.

"Venimos a compartir nuestras experiencias, a decirle al mundo entero que estamos aquí porque queremos defender nuestro planeta, queremos curarlo y cuidarlo.

"También estamos aquí para hacerle el reclamo legítimo a los gobiernos, al nuestro. Ya basta. Consúltenos, platiquémoslo, sean capaces de abrir sus corazones, las puertas de sus oficinas y escuchen porque nosotros tenemos propuestas y soluciones, armónicas con la Madre Tierra", enunció.

La Jornada

MIÉRCOLES 8 DE DICIEMBRE DE 2010 DIRECTORA GENERAL: CARMEN LIRA SAADE ■ DIRECTOR FUNDADOR: CARLOS PAYAN VELVER ■

Clamores críticos en la cumbre de Cancún

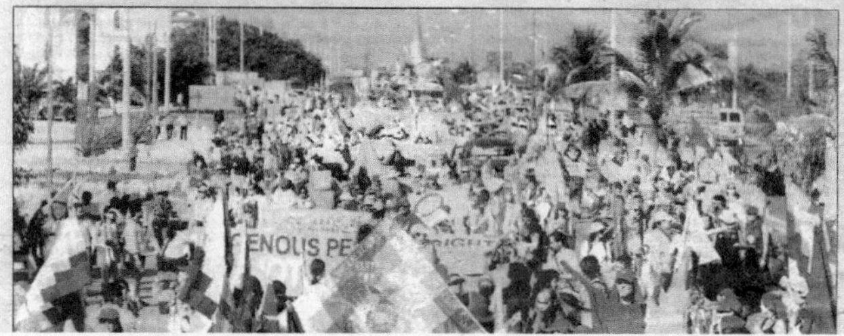

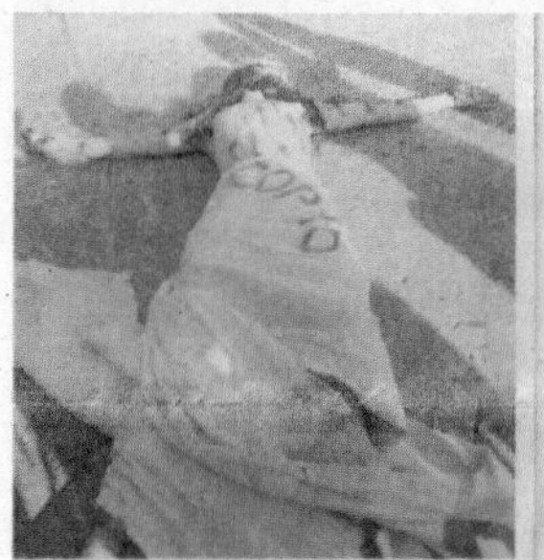

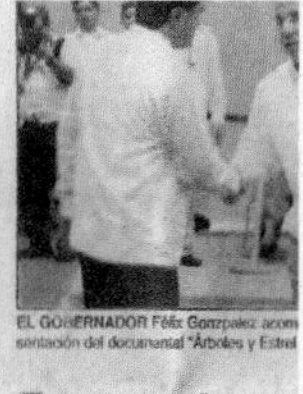

EL GOBERNADOR Félix González acom sentación del documental "Árboles y Estre

Emprende ac la Península c

VARILLAS/SÁNCHEZ/ROMERO

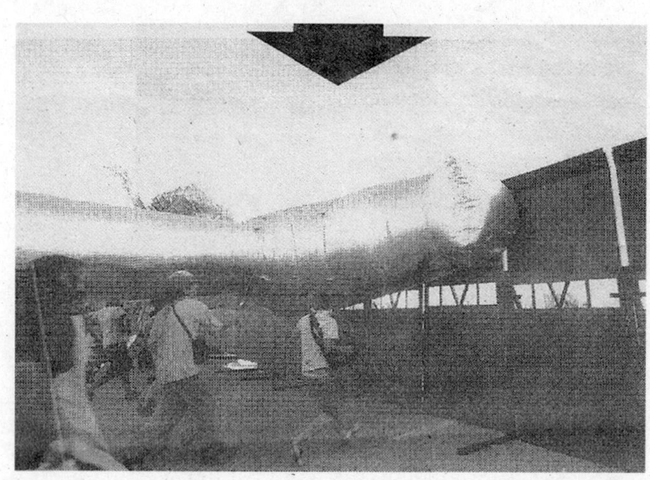

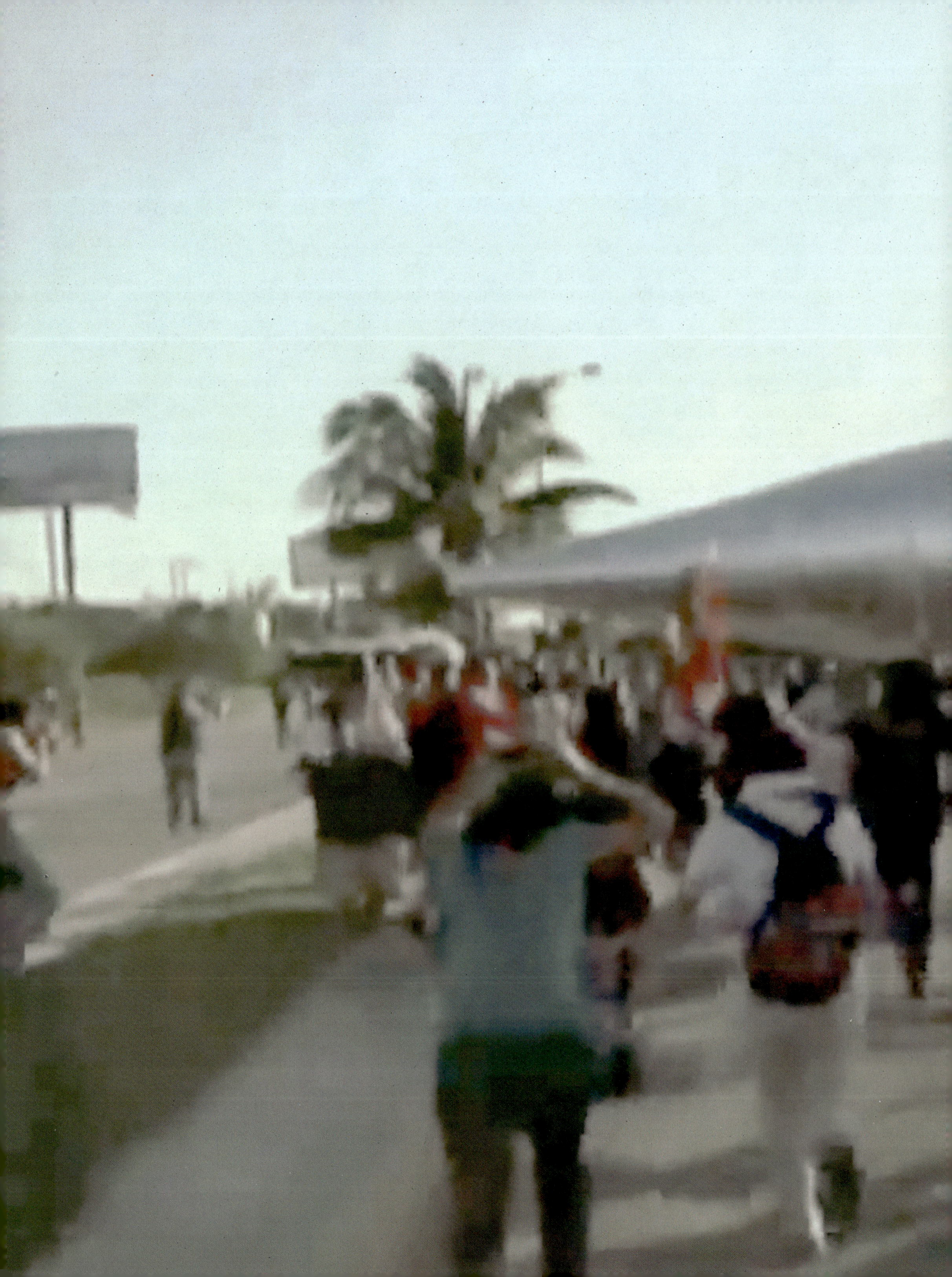

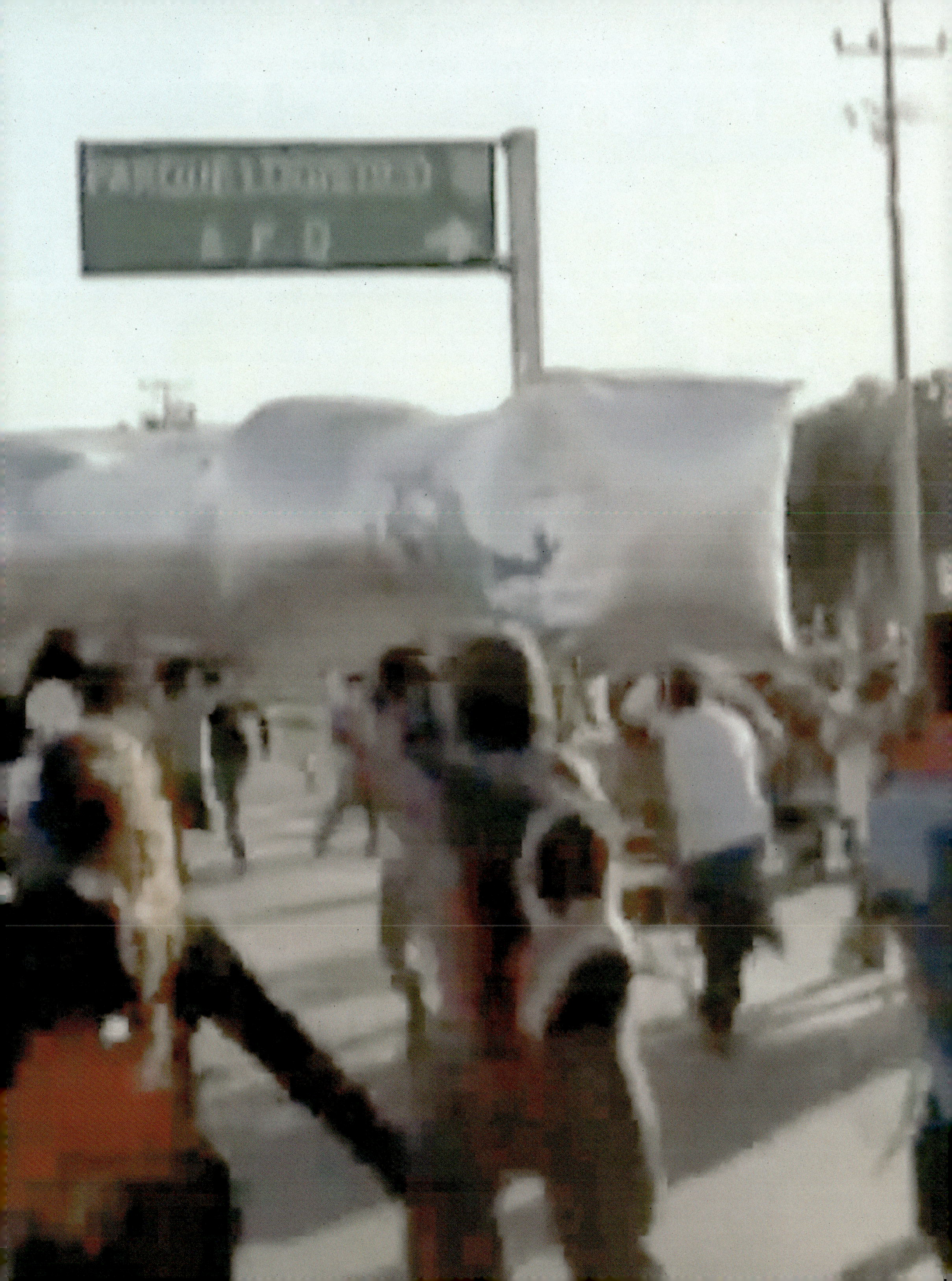

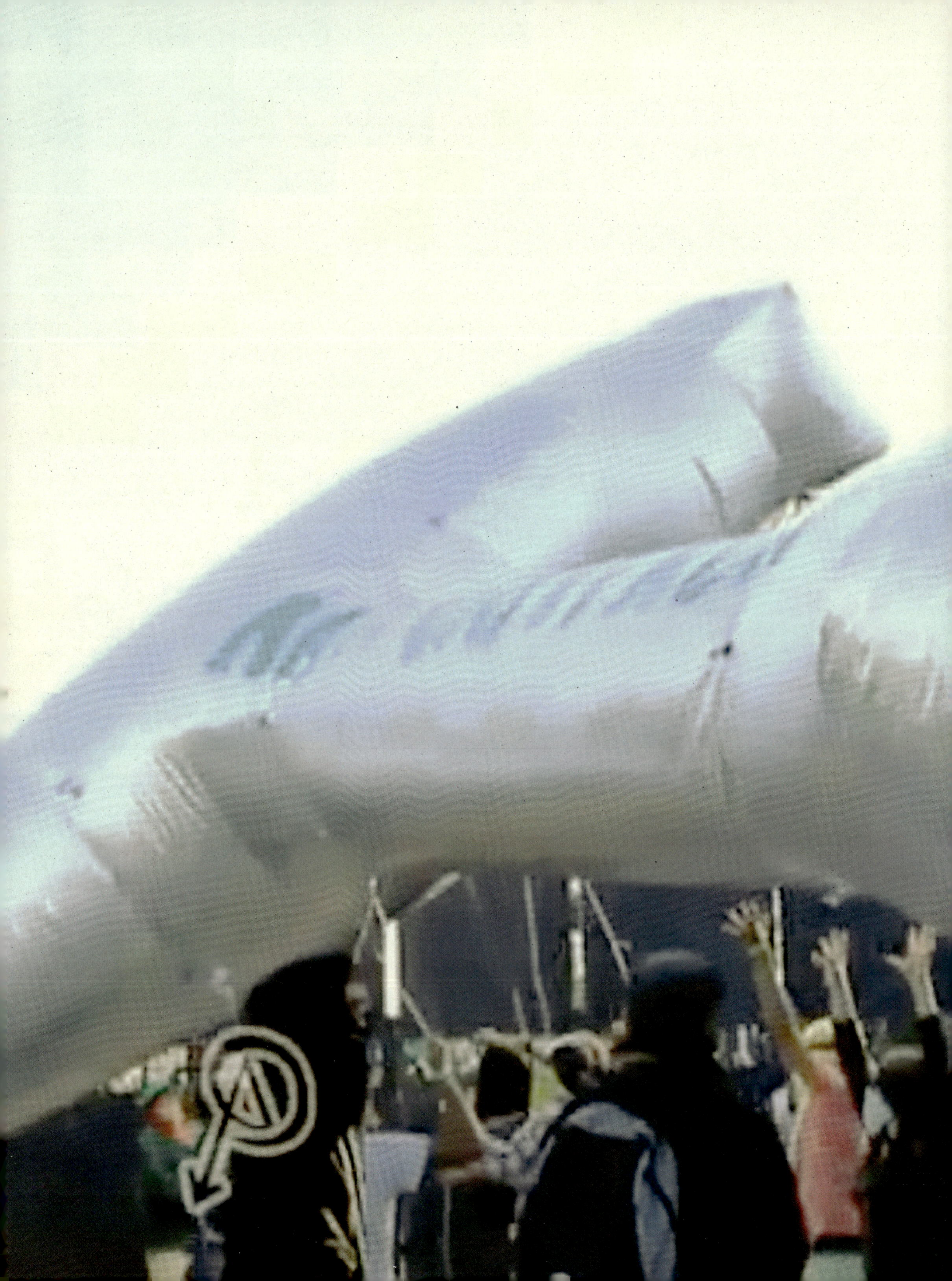

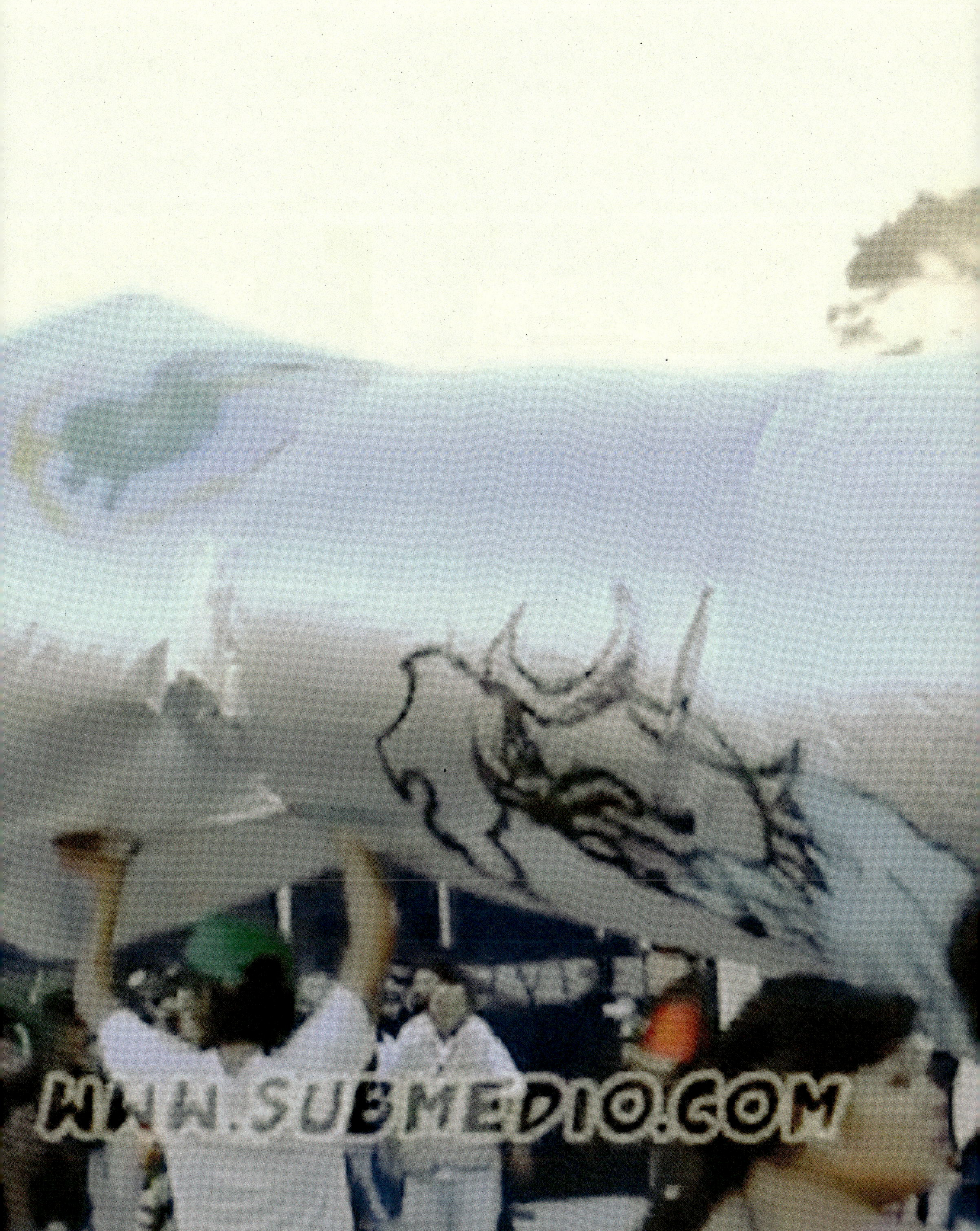
WWW.SUBMEDIO.COM

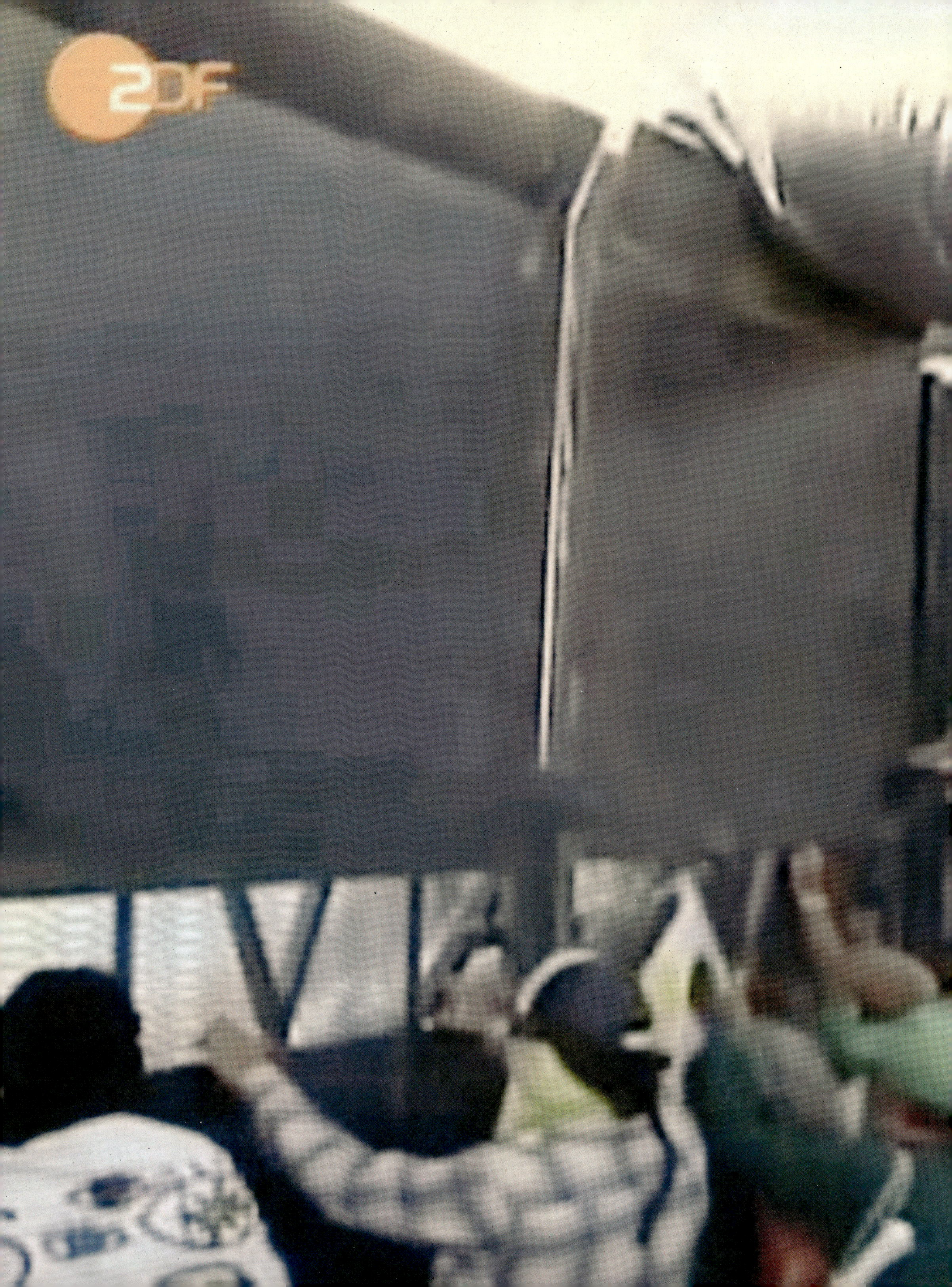
ZDF

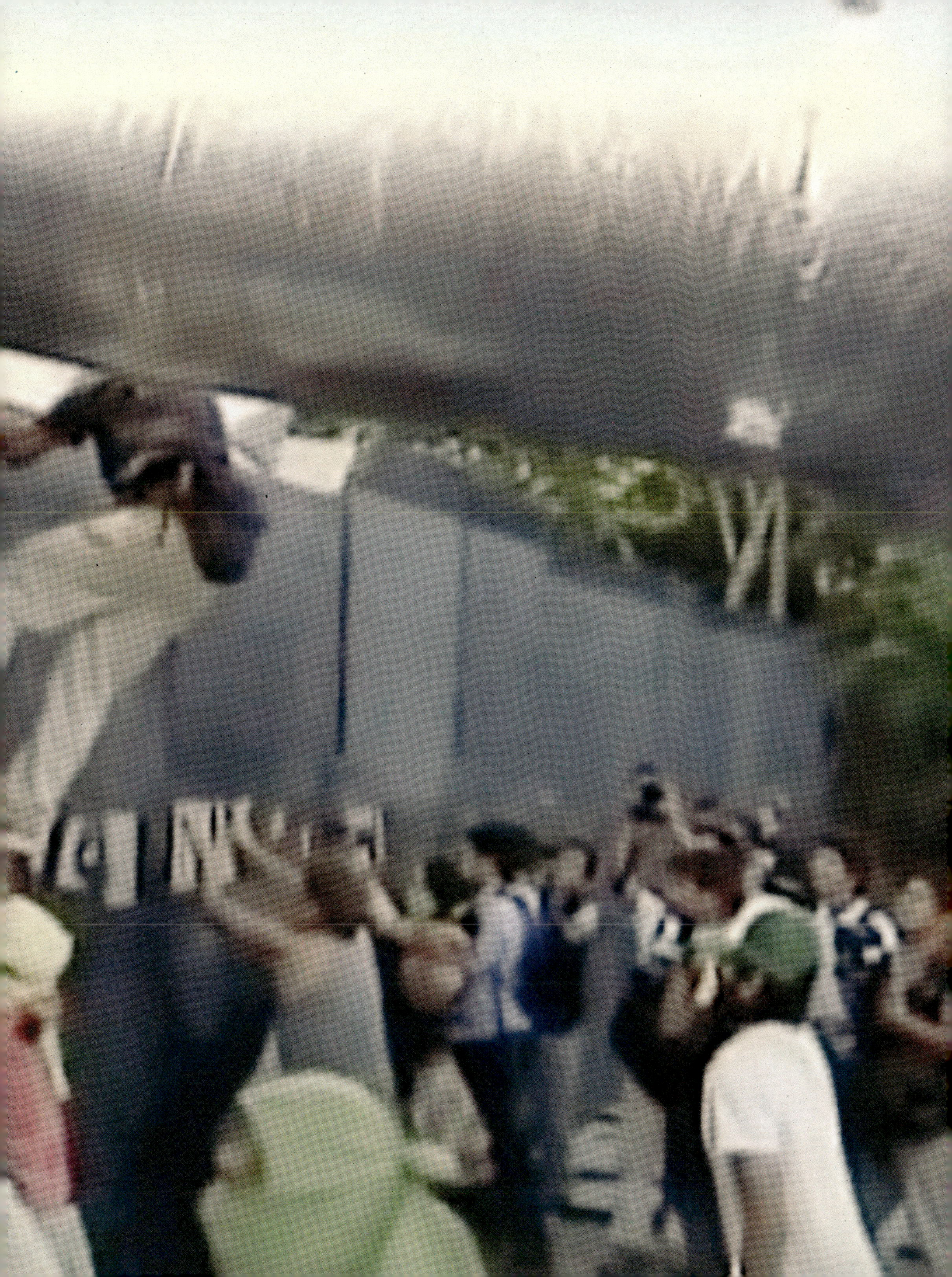

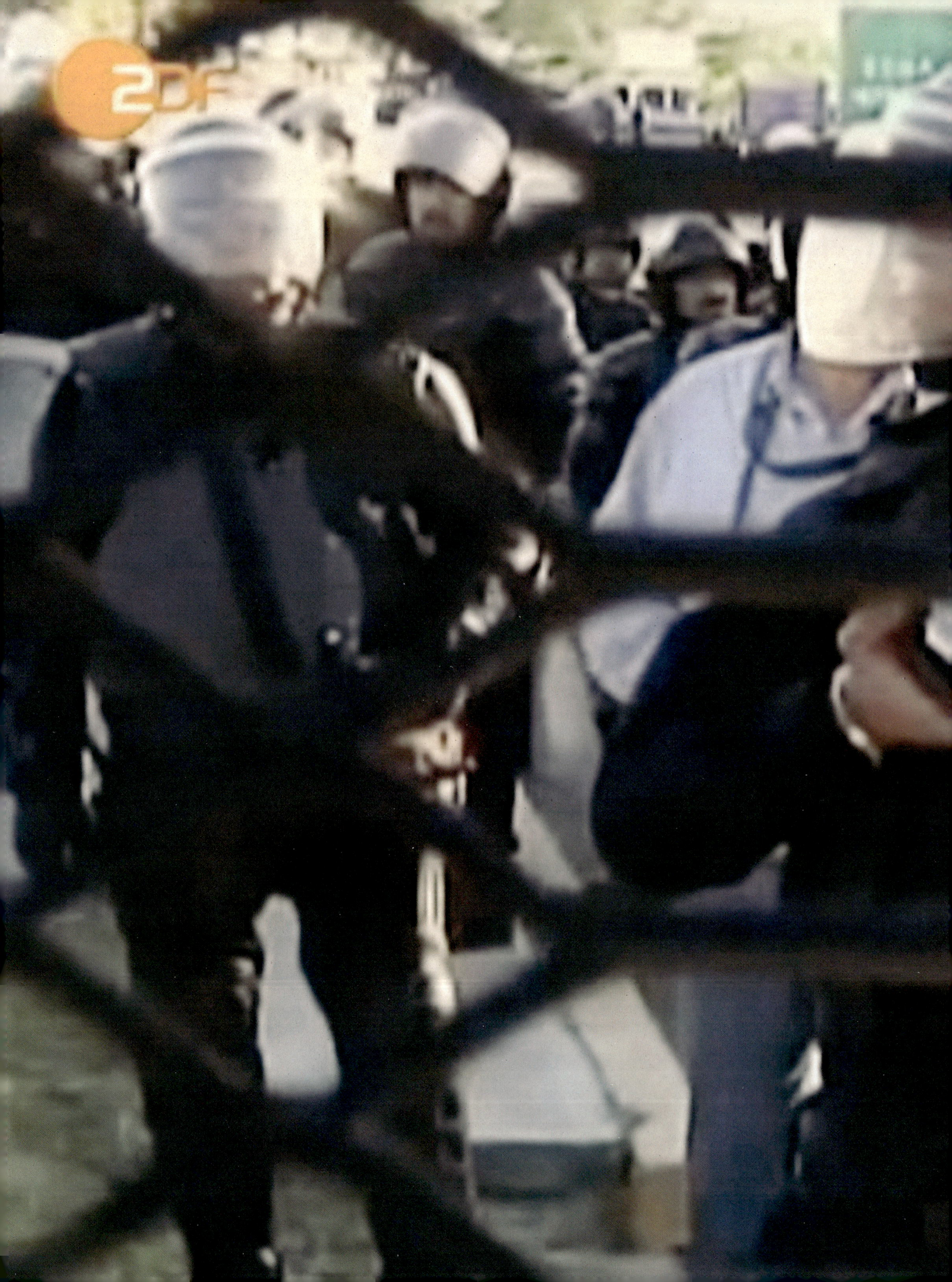
ZDF

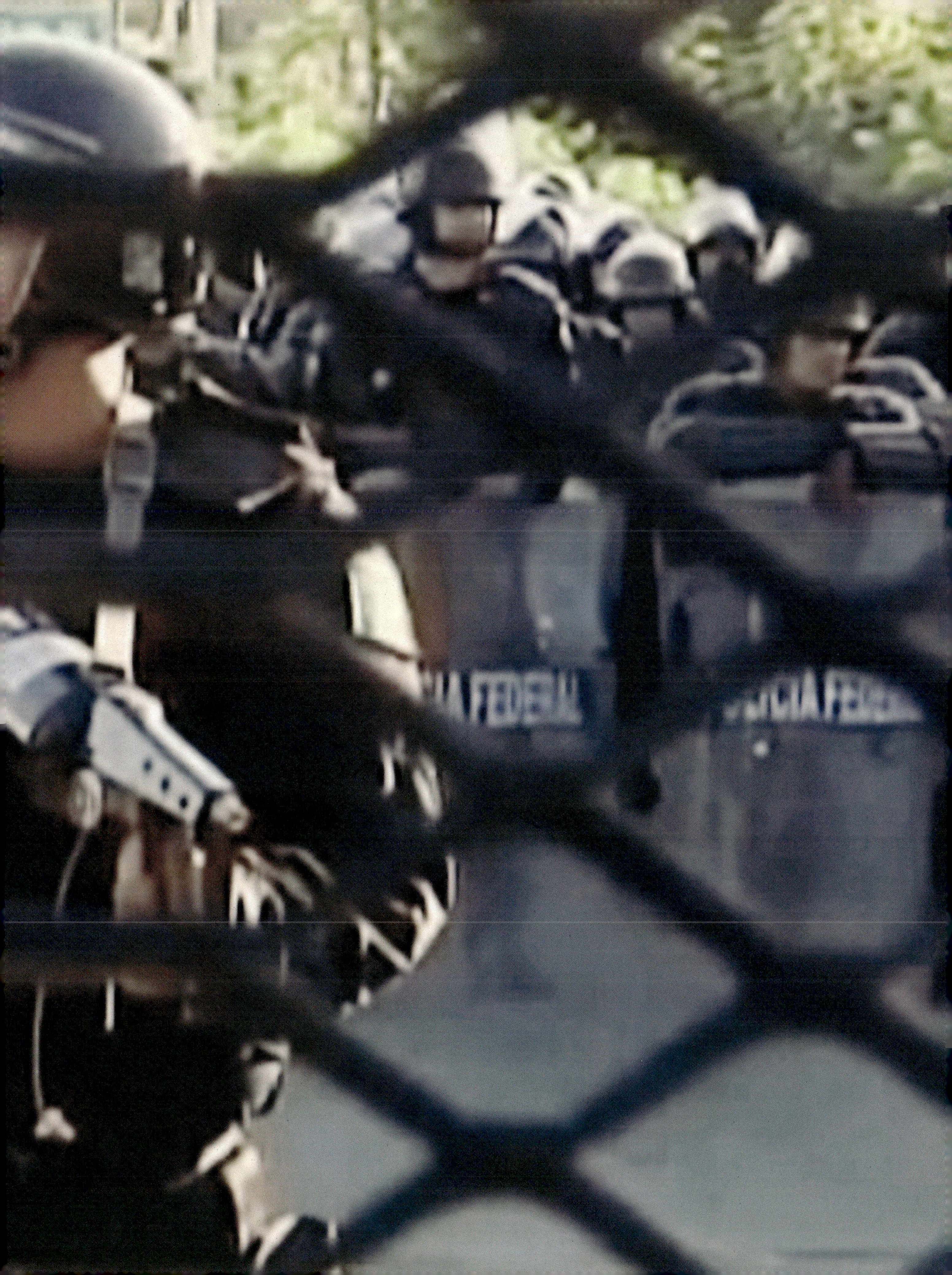
FEDERAL
FEDERAL

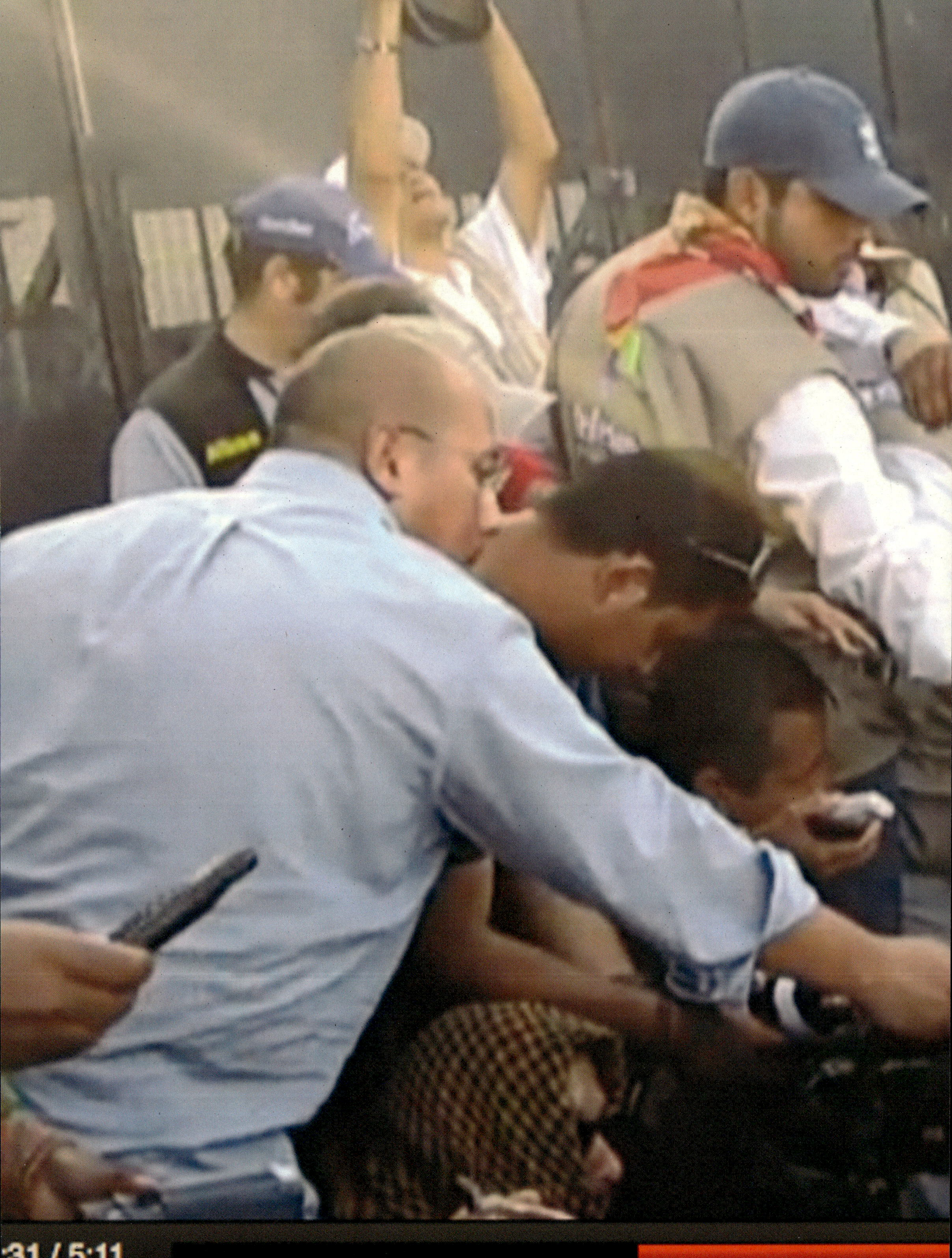
:31 / 5:11

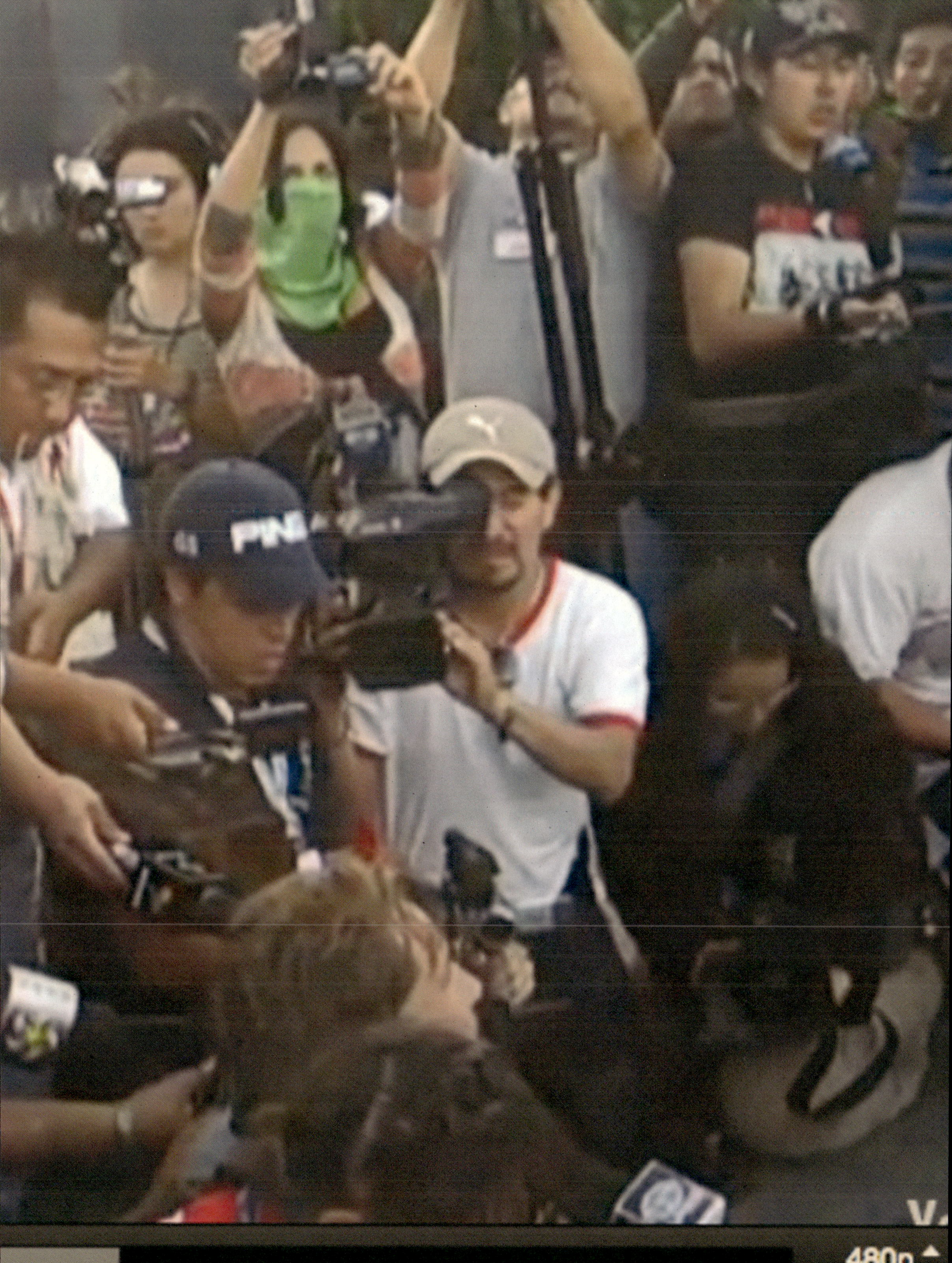
480p

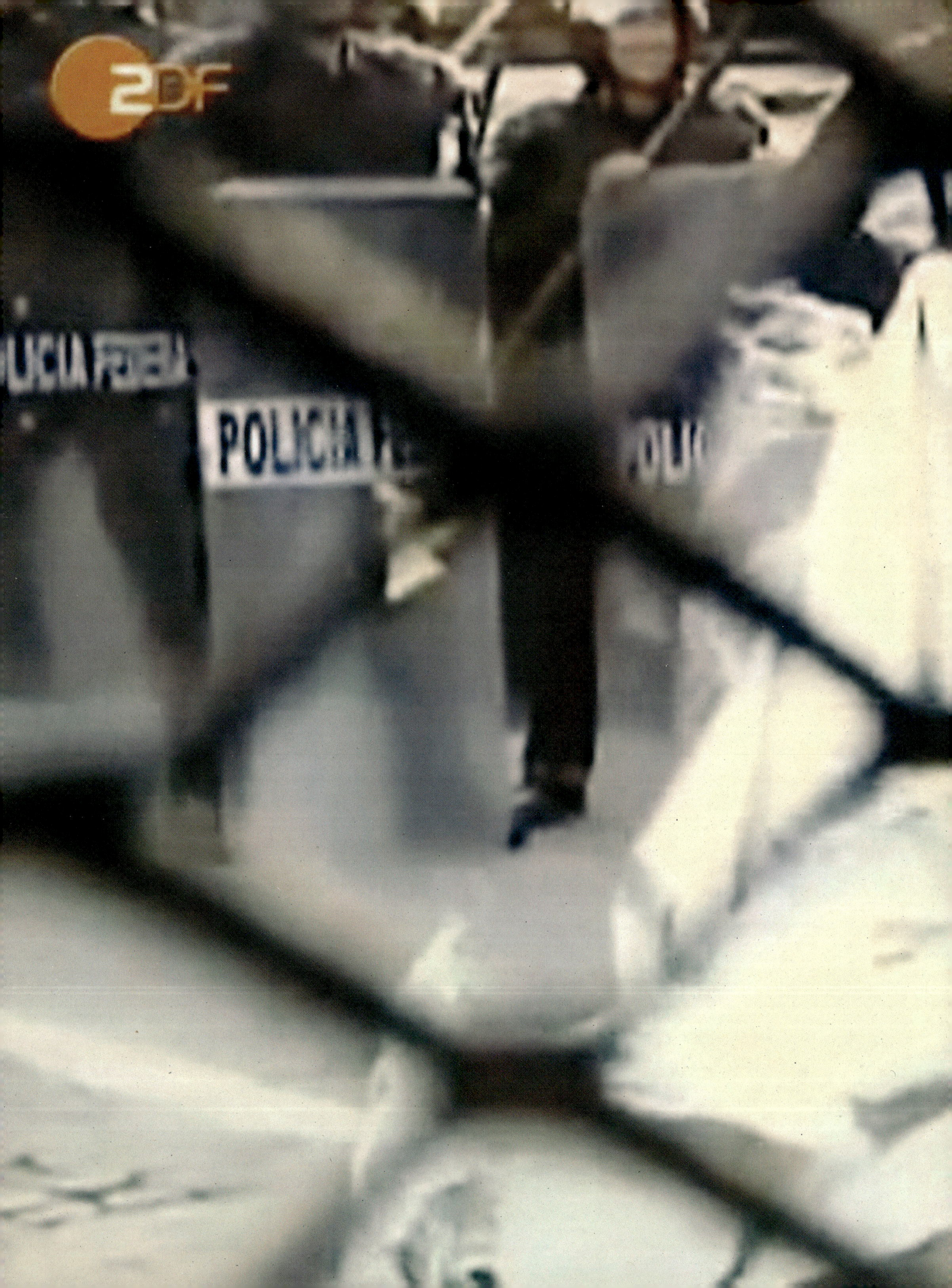
ZDF
POLICIA

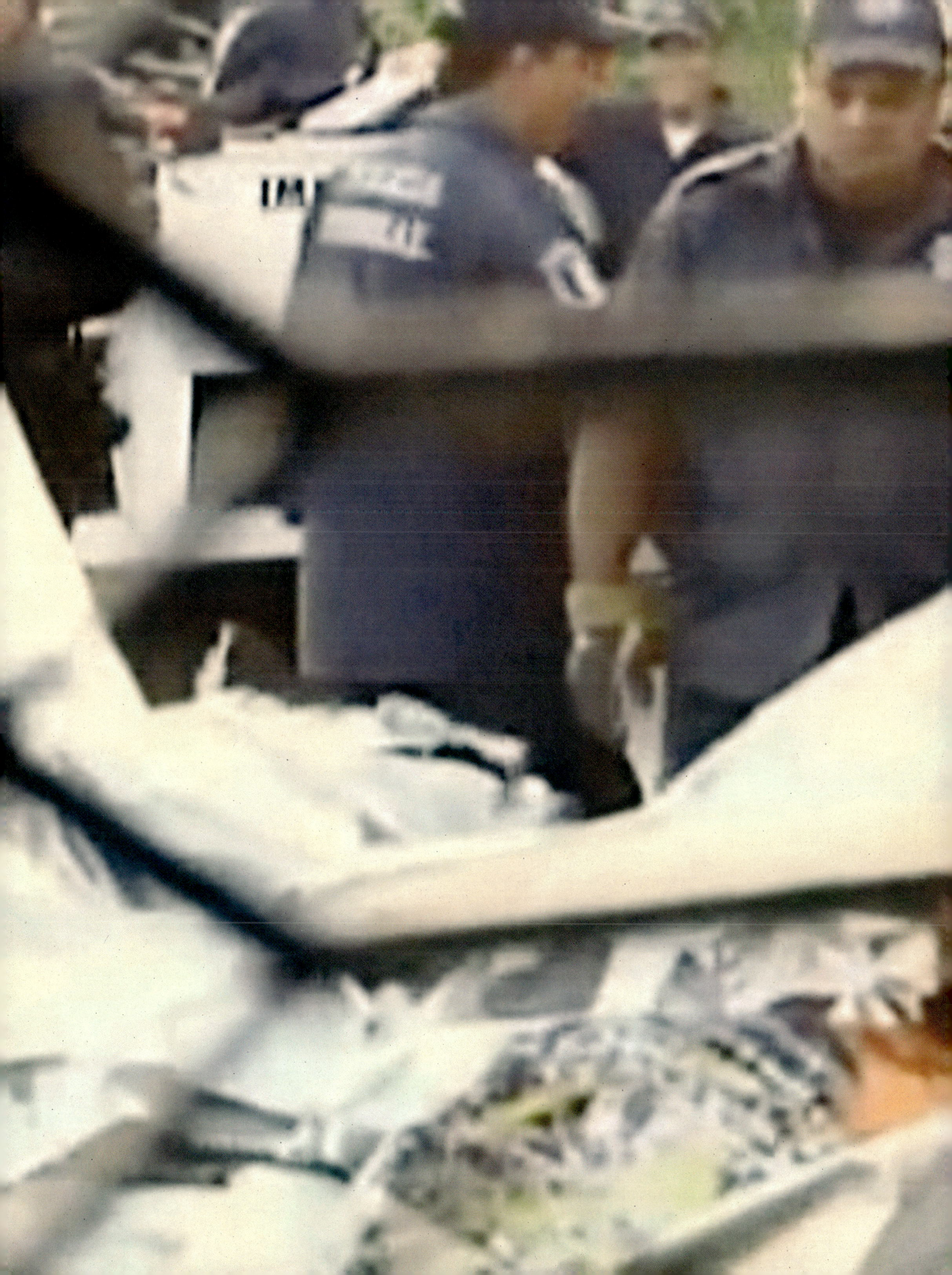

How to make an inflatable hammer Part 1

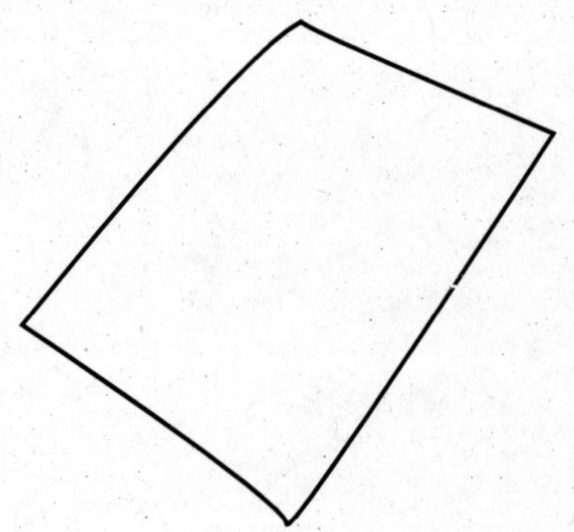

by Sarah Drain and Paul Pistorius

If all those instructions are followed carefully, the hammer will rise, from a little crumply silver heap to an eye blasting thing that has the ability of turning a protest into a spectacle.

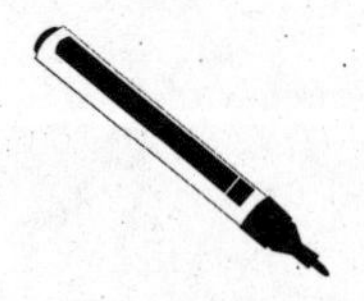

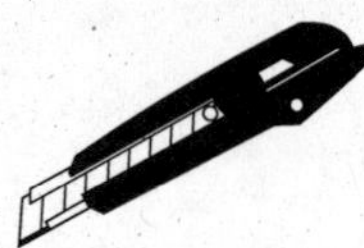

TOOLS AND MATERIALS
time and people (at least 2 workaholics)
clear head and precision
measurer, cutter, 3–4 sewing machines, markers
silver foil («Delta Reflex Luft–u. Dampfsperrbahn»!)
polyester sewing thread, two component epoxy superglue
silver or transparent adhesive tape
ventilator (we highly recommend the DV 6224 by ebm–papst)
2×12 V (recycled) car batteries
electricity wires & switch
2 m extractor hose

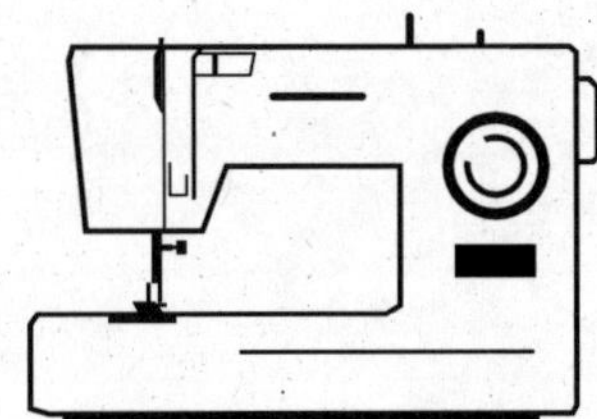

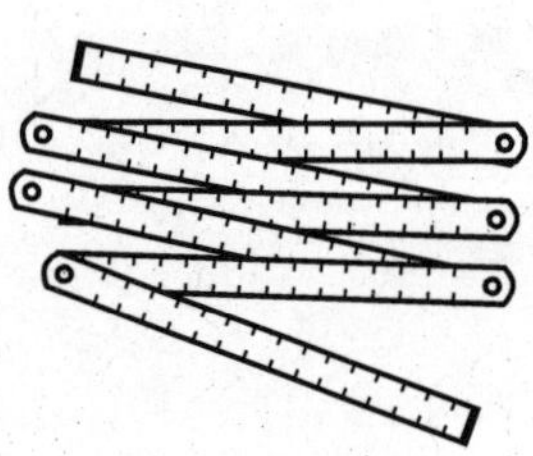

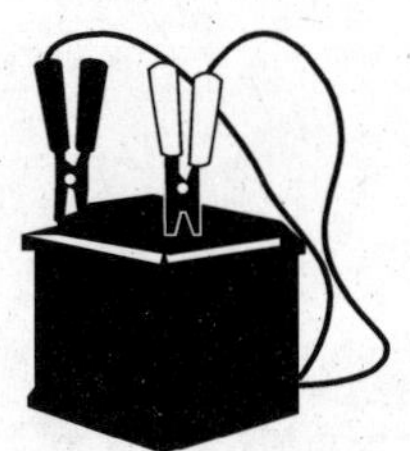

SEWING FROM A TO Q
Draw all the parts onto silver foil and cut them out.
Make tube like forms out of the B's, C's and D's.
Put the F's to the E's. The handle parts are ready for the head.
Put P, R and Q's together. For the middle part of the head start by closing part N in order to make a circle, then put this together with O, this goes onto L, which can than be put together with the M's.
Put J's to K's. Put H's to I's and attach G.
Put all parts together.
Don't forget to attach the flaps between the handle and head.
Flip the hammer around and attach part A.
You are finished.

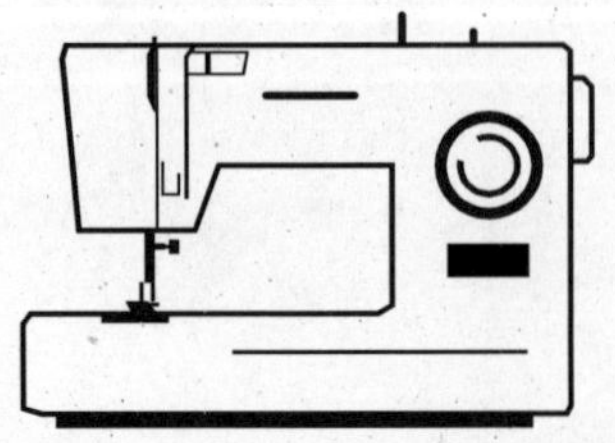